CONTENTS

The Centre → p. 62

The East → p. 74

Trips & Tours → p. 88

Road atlas → p. 118

MAPS IN THE GUIDEBOOK
(120 A1) Page numbers and coordinates refer to the road atlas
(0) Site/address located off the map. Coordinates are also given for places that are not marked on the road atlas
(U A1) Coordinates for the map of Havana inside the back cover

INSIDE BACK COVER: PULL-OUT MAP →

PULL-OUT MAP 🗺
(🗺 A–B 2–3) Refers to the removable pull-out map
(🗺 a–b 2–3) Refers to the additional inset maps on the pull-out map

The best MARCO POLO Insider Tips

Our top 15 Insider Tips

INSIDER TIP Rum old business

When the lights go on in the model version of the Central La Esperanza in the Havana Club museum and the miniature sugar train rumbles over the tracks, you can nearly smell the bubbling cauldrons of what will in the end become rum → **p. 37**

INSIDER TIP Strawberries and chocolate

Since the restaurant where Fresa y Chocolate was filmed reopened, you feel even more in a secret lodge of cineastes and gourmets. An experience of its own: the walk to the 3rd floor through the broken storeys → **p. 40**

INSIDER TIP Sweet seduction

There are so many delicacies based on Baracoa cocoa; admire the gourmet magic at the Museo de Chocolate in Habana vieja and take advantage to buy or taste, for instance, freshly made pralines or hot chocolate → **p. 41**

INSIDER TIP Salsa matinée

Is there anything better than dancing in Sunday dress at teatime in the open air to salsa rhythms? In Cuba this is called a matinée and takes place from about 5pm in the Jardines 1830 → **p. 45**

INSIDER TIP La Maison fashion show

The Caribbean beauties in tropical creations at the fashion show at La Maison induce outbursts of spontaneous shopping fever in the spectators → **p. 47**

INSIDER TIP Bohemian meeting place

Students, musicians, painters, literary types and other artists and artistes have chosen a restaurant with a pool right by the sea as their rendezvous: Don Cangrejo in Miramar in Havana → **p. 46**

INSIDER TIP River of adventure

Only 30 minutes from Varadero, catch a boat to dive deep into the primeval world of the Río Canimar (photo above) → **p. 57**

BEST OF ...

FOR FREE

● *The people's stage*
The best place to sit back and enjoy the sunset is on the little wall bordering the *Malecón* of Havana – 3 miles long and running along the sea: this meeting place with the city skyline as backdrop provides excellent 'urban theatre' – no ticket required (photo) → p. 33

● *Rhythms & rituals*
Drum roll in the *Callejón de Hamel:* on a Sunday, this small alleyway of Havana-Centro gives itself over to dance, worship of African deities and to offering tourists all kinds of magic stuff. A free spectacle, not only for Santería fans! → p. 35

● *Hall of pictures*
Why visit a museum if you can see contemporary art at the *Feria de los Artesanos* in a huge exhibition hall without paying the entrance fee? And a good number of works by new talent won't even break the bank → p. 41

● *Open-air concert*
Every evening from 10pm a big open-air music extravaganza of Cuban bands is staged on the *Escalinata* in Trinidad – and everybody is invited. Only the drinks at the bar have to be paid → p. 67

● *Paradise outside the front door*
For the inhabitants of the capital, the *Playas del Este* are like a gift of God: quickly reached by the tunnel and free for everybody, and that includes tourists of course. On a regular weekday you'll have magnificent beaches more or less to yourself
→ p. 48

● *Che for ever*
Pay your respects to the philosopher of the 'New Man': thousands of Che fans from all over the world have already visited his last place of rest, the *Museo Memorial del Ernesto Che Guevara* in Santa Clara – and it's free to boot. This is surely what the man himself would have wanted ... → p. 70

●●●● Dots in guidebook refer to 'Best of ...' tips

● *Gifted dancers*

At Havana's *Cabaret Tropicana* long-legged beauties – the best dancers in Cuba – and their partners enchant the world with the rhythms of Latin America. If you want to understand Cuba, make sure you experience them once → **p. 46**

● *Taste of Cuba*

Cool like the crushed ice, the soda water and the fresh mint, sweet as Cuban sugar and enchanting like light Cuban rum, that's what a real mojito should taste like. The top place to sample one is Havana's *Bodeguita del Medio* → **p. 41**

● *Houses of song*

Clear the stage for son, salsa, bolero or trova – in Cuba, the *casas de la trova* ('song houses') are places of worship, where people show reverence when dancing or just listening to the musicians. One with a particularly good ambience is in Santiago de Cuba → **p. 83, 85**

● *Holy smoke*

Cuba boasts the world's best tobacco plantations, and the aroma of a true 'Havana' sets cigar lovers on the path to ecstasy. Visit the factories of *Partagás* in Havana or *Donatién* in Pinar del Río to watch how they are made (photo) → **p. 41, 52**

● *Culture for everybody*

In Cuban life, education counts. Art and culture have their home in the *casa de cultura*. These cultural centres are open to visitors too. In Camagüey, for instance, they exhibit work by local artists → **p. 64**

● *Revolution in the museum*

Cuba wouldn't be the same without its revolutionary museums. In Santa Clara, Santiago de Cuba and Havana in particular, the government extols the achievements of its heroes with museums and memorials. The country's youngsters however, are losing interest ... → **p. 37, 71, 83**

● *The real national anthem*

There can't be many who don't know *Guantanamera,* Cuba's world-famous ballad? The lyrics, written by a national hero, the poet José Martí, honour a peasant woman from Guantánamo, and Fernández Díaz set them to music → **p. 77**

ONLY IN

BEST OF ...

● **Vintage studies**

The pre-revolutionary automobiles assembled in the *Museo del Automóvil* in Havana are real treasures. A visit here will also help you identify the vintage cars still circulating on Cuba's roads → p. 36

● **Papa's retreat**

A visit to 'Papa' Hemingway's former finca *La Vigía* is travelling back in time – could there have been a better place to write than that? In Hemingway's time, the finca was not yet situated between main roads like today (photo) → p. 48

● **Trip into the underworld**

Down in the cave, the weather outside doesn't matter: the vaults and corridors of the *Cuevas de Bellamar* in Matanzas form an intricate subterranean system. The intrepid grab a pit lamp and explore unlit corners → p. 100

● **Worlds of faith**

The confusing and disturbing world of the Cuban Santería and secret societies is excellently displayed in the *Museo Histórico de Guanabacoa*. For all the explanations, the exhibits speak their own language → p. 48

● **Chandeliers and mahogany**

Noblesse oblige... to lead an upper-crust lifestyle – the extent of which can be admired in the former Palacio Brunet, today's *Museo Romántico* in Trinidad → p. 72

● **Wax figures**

Cuban's only *wax works* is located a bit off the beaten track, but if you're in Bayamo, don't miss saying hello to life-size likenesses of Benny Moré, Compay Segundo and Ernesto 'Che' Guevara → p. 86

RAIN

RELAX AND CHILL OUT
Take it easy and spoil yourself

● **Sitting comfortably?**
Sometimes only an open-top Chrysler Bel Air with soft leather seating will do. This kind of 1950s cruiser picks up guests for relaxing tours of the city in front of the *Parque Central* hotel in Havana → **p. 34**

● **Serious pampering**
'Sauna, sensual showers, sun' is the promise made to spa fans by the *Sol Río de Luna y Mares* and *Paradisus Sol Río Resort & Spa* resorts on Playa Esmeralda (photo) → **p. 80**

● **Full steam ahead**
Lean back and enjoy the view: daily at 9.30am the *tren de vapor* steam train leaves the Estación de Toro in Trinidad to head into the valley of the sugar mills (Valle de los Ingenios) and back → **p. 73**

● **Diplomatic status**
You'll be in good company, guaranteed: in the *Club Havana* lounge between diplomats in the sauna, on the small beach or around the jacuzzi. And for tourists the pleasure isn't even that expensive → **p. 45**

● **Fine baths**
Let yourself be pampered: at the *Cayo Ensenacho Royal SPA* with its 130 sq m/1400 sq ft spa area, everything is top quality: Turkish baths, massages, manicures? Close your eyes and enjoy → **p. 71**

● **Above the rooftops**
The best bit about the historic *Hotel Raquel* is the roof terrace. All we need now is a *cafecito* – or is it time already for a mojito? *The* place to lean back and enjoy Havana's roof-top landscape → **p. 43**

● **Paseo colonial: two horse-power**
The horses are harnessed, the coachman is sitting on his box: your job is to lean back, and you're away! In Old Havana it's easy to find a gentle carriage drive: they wait for passengers at Parque Central → **p. 39**

INTRODUCTION

DISCOVER CUBA!

Cuba has long since joined the ranks of top Caribbean destinations. Far over two million visitors arrive every year, yet by no means all its beautiful beaches and islands have been opened up to tourism. As the Caribbean's largest country, Cuba offers absolutely inexhaustible opportunities for sun-hungry and adventurous holidaymakers.

The fascination that Cuba exerts on the visitor goes much beyond tourist attractions, and most of all that's to do with *socialismo tropical* – 'tropical socialism'. A good number of the student revolt generation of 1968 meet their old ideals of a more just society here. Cuban society after all is the work of Fidel Castro and Ernesto 'Che' Guevara, the idols fêted at that time. Of course, contradictions between high ideals and the much less shiny reality, which are apparent on Cuba too, hit those who have a retro vision of politics harder than the apolitical holidaymaker. Intellectuals will love or hate Cuba – but the country will leave nobody indifferent.

Photo: Varadero

For those who still remember old-style communism in the former Soviet bloc, Cuba is an encounter of the special kind. They know the 'system', the advantages and disadvantages, understand the 'language', as it were, even without speaking a lot of Spanish. And everybody asks themselves: what next, Cuba – after the Castro era? Whether or not you think much about politics, and regardless of whether you are well-travelled, and no matter what your age group – Cuba will not leave you indifferent. It might be love at second sight. Without any doubt there is much that will stay in your mind: e.g. that the streets and countryside are not blighted by rubbish, that the people might not have much but are proud, with a high level of education and full of the joy of life.

That said, socialism certainly hasn't turned Cuba into a wealthy country – the economic embargo by the USA being one of the reasons. Yet no visitor will feel like in a Third World country. Children working as shoeshine boys? Not here. Women who have no say in public life? Not in Cuba. Sick and crippled beggars? Those too are the exception here. In order to see the true Cuba though, you'll have to take a look beyond the façade of a country forever struggling to survive economically, and meet its people. There are several ways to do this: tours around the island by bus and rental car, or participation in programmes run by specialised operators: hikes with Cuban guides or a combination of salsa and Spanish classes with Cuban teachers.

Glimpses of real life

1000 BC – AD 1000
Arawak Indians arrive

1492
Columbus takes possession of Cuba for the Spanish crown

1553
Havana becomes capital and the main shipyard for New Spain

1762
England conquers Havana. Shortly after, Cuba is swapped for Spanish Florida

1789–1820
Flow of refugees from Haiti. Cuba becomes the largest exporter of sugar

Colonial charm beneath palm trees: Trinidad

So... discover Cuba! Havana of course is a must. Traditionally always more showy and cosmopolitan than any other Caribbean capital, today the 'City of Columns', as Cuban author Alejo Carpentier called Havana, is the nation's pride. Habana vieja, the old quarter, in particular, is full of tourists from Europe, Japan, Latin America and the US, since Cuban exiles living there are allowed to visit their family, i.e. aunts, uncles, first and second cousins, without restric-

> **Havana – capital of the Caribbean**

tions. And that means: as long and as often as they like. However, during their stay they are only allowed to spend a daily amount of US dollars equivalent to the current expenses allowance of the US Foreign Office (at the time of going to press 179

1868–78
First War of Independence against Spain

1895–98
Second War of Independence; leading after US intervention to dependence on the USA

1902
Cuba becomes a republic

1902–58
Sugar export boom in the World War I. US-controlled puppet presidents, the last of whom was dictator F. Batista

1953–59
Victory of the revolution under Fidel Castro – after time spent in prison and years of exile in Mexico

US$). Previously, decades of the US embargo against communist Cuba meant that exiled Cubans were only allowed to travel to Cuba once a year. Exiled Cubans sending money from the US to support their families are no longer subject to an upper limit (which at the end stood at 1200 dollars).

Waterfalls, limestone mountains, royal palms and magnificent beaches

Not far from the capital, gentle mountain ranges rise, with bubbling springs and orchids blossoming next to waterfalls. Hiking trails open up a biosphere reserve with its rich flora and fauna. A few miles on, guests staying at the panorama hotels enjoy the view of the Valle de Viñales from their terrace. In the morning ground mist wafts around the humpy limestone mountains known as mogotes – an image of mystical beauty. The Valle de Viñales is considered one of the world's best tobacco-growing areas. That again is followed by what seems to be the end of the world: the Guanahacabibes peninsula with the diving destination of María La Gorda. East of Havana the beaches of the capital await, the Yumurí valley and Cuba's most important beach resort: Varadero with its long broad beach. In the southeast of Havana you can discover the Caribbean's largest swamp, the Ciénaga de Zapata, a virgin forest criss-crossed by canals, lagoons and rivers and inhabited by crocodiles, manatees and birds.

All this however is only for starters. After the 'head' of Havana and its surroundings, the Cuban mainland extends some 620 miles eastwards in the direction of Haiti. One holiday is not nearly enough to discover it all, even if you bridge the longest distances by plane. One wonderful destination is only accessible by air anyway: the coral island of Cayo Largo with its dream beach. Like a dorsal spine, the Autopista Central runs along the centre of the long body of the island, adding one provincial capital after the other to the string, as it were. The first as you head east is Santa Clara, whose capture by Che Guevara on 1 January 1959 marked the victory of the revolution. Since the tireless revolutionary found his last resting place there in the Museo Memorial del Ernesto Che Guevara, the town has become a site of pilgrimage for all Che fans. It is also the gateway to Cuba's latest holiday destination, the Cayos de la Herradura, first and foremost the Cayo Santa María. The new streams of tourists have also awoken pretty colonial Remedios on the way to the Cayos from its Sleeping Beauty slumber.

1960
The US economic embargo starts to kick in; the USSR becomes trading partner number one

1991–94
Economic crisis induced by the collapse of the USSR. A tourist infrastructure is set up

2008
After 49 years as head of state, a very sick Fidel Castro transfers the office to his brother Raúl.

2010/11
Raúl Castro loosens some bans, allowing Cubans to enter tourist hotels, possess a mobile phone and to drive a taxi on a self-employed basis

Primeval river landscape in eastern Cuba

In the south, Sancti Spíritus is the gateway to the Escambray mountain range: cool conifer forests, reservoir lakes, deep valleys, hidden waterfalls in the backcountry, and along the ocean the towns of Trinidad und Cienfuegos. Don't fail to walk through the cobbled alleyways of Trinidad and enjoy the views from the municipal museum's viewpoint across the rooftops of this colonial town, which has been almost entirely preserved. Beyond Sancti Spíritus, Cuba changes into a wide plain of

The mystical east

cattle pastures with scattered palms, under the vault of a tropical sky. At irregular intervals you'll find towns such as Ciego de Ávila, Camagüey, Las Tunas and Holguín, vibrant provincial capitals which lead their own busy lives far from Havana. Again and again roads down to the sea invite drivers to take detours to the northern coast: to the new tourist oasis of Cayo Santa María or the holiday enclaves of Cayo Coco and Cayo Guillermo, to bays and beaches, flamingo lagoons and mangrove forests, to small ports and the holiday centres of Playa Santa Lucía and Guardalavaca. At its eastern end Cuba really dishes up the treats: with a wide river plain and the Sierra Maestra, rising to the country's highest peak. In the shelter of this mountain range, the rebels once prepared their revolution. Fidel Castro was born in Oriente, and his parental estate is only a day trip away from Holguín. The east also harbours Cuba's oldest colonial towns: Baracoa and lively Santiago de Cuba. The east is the bedrock of the country, spiced with a good pinch of Afro-Cuban temperament. On top of that, nature has blessed the region with the primeval Alturas de Baracoa – better known as Humboldt National Park. In 2001, Unesco added the park to its list of World Natural Heritage sites.

WHAT'S HOT

1 Bump and grind

El Perreo Dancing is one of the great Cuban passions. The sound of the moment is the perreo – young, wild and pretty sexy. Learn the first moves in the *Academia de Baile Ritmo Cubano (information from www.cuba-plus.com)*, and apply what you've learned at the trendy *El Chévere* club *(Parque Almendares, Havana)*. Before you travel, bring the sound into your home on-line *(www.perreo.co.uk)*.

Cuba by bike

Travel like the locals Discover the country the way the Cubans do: at a leisurely pedal pace. *Bicycles Crossing Borders* sends unused bicycles from Canada to Cuba to support the local population. Renting a bike from them means supporting the project at the same time *(in the Metropolitano building, San Juan de Dios, Havana, www.bikesto cuba.org)*. A tour including bike hire, guide and ac-commodation can be booked through *Gap Adventures (www.gapadventures.com, photo)* or *Cubamar (www.cubamarviajes.cu)*.

2

Sound of Cuba

3

From Alamar into the world Cuban rap is the sound of the underground – small wonder, as the singers' lyr-ics take no prisoners. The music has its origins in Havana's prefab dormitory town of Alamar. One of the strong-est voices of the scene is *Telmary Díaz (www.my space.com/telmary)*. The duo *Ogguere (www. myspace.com/oggueremusic)* and rapper *Ku-mar (www.myspace.com/kumarmate)* are examples of rap cubano. The best chance to watch the new generation of rappers perform live is at *Barbaram Pepito's Bar (Ave. 26, Havana)*.

Domino effect

Clickety-clack You can hear this sound everywhere on Cuba's streets: the clattering of dominoes. Games are going on at any time of day or night, but you'll stand the best chance of being invited to a round on Havana's Plaza de Armas. A game in Calle Padre Pico offers new perspectives in both senses of the word. From the stepped street connecting the Upper and Lower Town of Santiago de Cuba, you can see all the way to the mountains. If you've been bitten by the domino bug, consider purchasing a set at Havana's *Fería de Artesanía* crafts market to take home *(Calle Tacón)*. But be careful, as the love of dominoes doesn't stop after death. On the *Cementerio Colón* you'll find the grave of the 'Domino Dead', a local woman who died of a heart attack during a game. The sequence of her last match has been immortalised on her tomb. Today, gamesters visit her grave for that little bit of extra luck *(entrance Zapata/Calle 12, Havana)*.

4

Art from nothing

5

Recycling Making a virtue out of necessity. Lucía Fernández for one turns trash into sculptures. And very successfully at that: her works even made it onto the runway of the *Art and Style Fashion* show in Havana, which took place as part of *Artecorte (www.artecorte. net)*. The *Guerra de la Paz* group creates impressive sculptures from old clothing. Their works in bonsai or snake shapes enjoy international success *(www.guerradelapaz.com)*. In Angel Ramírez' works, old materials finish up on the walls as two-dimensional paintings *(www.amramirez.com, photo)*. The *Servando* gallery supports local artists *(Calle 23, Havana)*.

IN A NUTSHELL

ARCHITECTURE

Many of the houses in *Habana vieja* still date back from the time of the neo-baroque style which manifested itself during the 18th century sugar boom in the form of ornate entrances, marble floors and columns. For protection against humidity the walls were tiled and mahogany wood was used for ceilings and banister rails. The older balconies were made from wood; later the fashion changed to stone balconies with cast-iron decorative grilles *(rejas)*. Multicoloured leaded glass soon became the fashion in fanlights above doors opening to patios with airy galleries leading to high-ceilinged rooms. In the early 20th century these splendid old edifices were joined by opulent art nouveau, art deco and Bauhaus buildings. The oldest house on Cuba (1522) is the Casa de Velázquez in Santiago. Here you can see an excellent example of the colonial Spanish style of architecture featuring a *patio* gallery fitted with ventilation grilles. *Bohíos*, Indian huts built from clay and wooden sticks, have survived architecturally as tourist restaurants and bungalows.

BEACHES

Some 300 beaches take up over 365 miles of the over 3500-mile-long coast: most have white fine sand, like the famous Playas Varadero and Guardalavaca in the north, or those on the islands of Cayos Las Brujas, Ensenachos and Santa María or Cayos Coco und Guillermo. The most beautiful beaches of the

Photo: Cienfuegos, Parque Martí

From architecture to sugar: what newcomers should know in order to see beyond Cuba's tropical façade

south are Playa Ancón near Trinidad, the Playa Bacanao off Santiago de Cuba and the one at Cayo Largo.

CHE GUEVARA

By birth, he was Argentine. And in the end he did get close his country of birth, restlessly driven by the idea of revolutionising the world. On 8 October 1967 Ernesto 'Che' Guevara was captured in the Bolivian region of Oriente and executed the next day in the school of the village of La Higuera, on government or-

ders. His mortal remains were only found in 1997, hastily buried below a runway. In the same year Fidel Castro had them brought to Santa Clara, where Che Guevara's victory over Batista's troops once sealed the victory of the revolution. With his idea of the 'New Man' forsaking material values, Che became an idol, and his photograph, reproduced millions of times, an icon for the generation of 1968 all over the world. In 2008 Steven Soderbergh erected a cinematic monument to him with the epic Che – Revolución.

ECONOMY

Raúl Castro continues to hold on to the ideology of a socialist planned economy. Since the loss of the Soviet Union as a trading partner, the main pillars of the economy have been tourism, with some 2.5 million visitors in 2010, and

In 1791, Cuba was the world's largest sugar producer, and in the early 20th century the main supplier to the US. After the revolution Cuba kept the Soviet Union in sugar. Today, it is offered as a barter commodity with Russia, China and new trading partners in Europe and

Crocodile in the Ciénaga de Zapata biosphere reserve

the export of medical services (doctors, skilled medical staff). New sources of income have been created too, amongst them cultivating pineapple and citrus fruit, exporting fruit juices and breeding prawns. Thanks to trade treaties with EU countries, Canada and a few countries in Latin America, the markets for sugar, formerly the main export, which now only makes up 25 per cent of agricultural production, are stabilising somewhat –as are those for tobacco, cocoa and coffee. Cuba is also the world's largest supplier of nickel. So far, the US has not loosened the trade embargo from the 1960s.

Introduced by Columbus, sugar cane has only been cultivated on a large scale in Cuba since the late 18th century. In order to take part in the sugar boom, large swathes of the country were deforested.

Canada. The harvest *(zafra)* takes place in late November and May (at the beginning and end of the dry season), mainly by hand.

ENVIRONMENT

Over the past few years, the state has focussed on implementing promises to protect the environment, including ever more of its numerous intact tropical ecosystems. Overall there are 263 nature reserves today, amongst them the national parks of *Alejandro de Humboldt* and *Desembarco del Granma* in the east, *Limones-Tuabaquey* in the centre at Camagüey, *Jardines de la Reina* (with over 4000 islands) off the southern coast, the *Valle de Viñales* in the west and the *Peninsula Guanahacabibes* in the southwest. Unesco has given six culti-

vated landscapes the status of biosphere reserves. Some cover all or part of the national parks, as on the Guanahacabibes peninsula. All in all, nearly a quarter of Cuba enjoys protected status. For more information see: *www.turnatcuba.com*

bays of the Ciénaga de Zapata. In this Unesco biosphere reserve a prehistoric fish species has survived too: the manjuarí, estimated to be 150 million years old. Divers can look forward to over 900 species of fish.

FAUNA

Ornithologists in particular wax lyrical about Cuba's bird life: of the 350 species listed, 300 are migratory birds and 25 endemic species such as the tocororo, which was declared Cuba's national bird for its blue, red and white plumage. Cuba has 54 species of mammals, amongst them the large rodent *Jutía conga* living in the mountain forests. One of the 42 reptile species is the harmless Santa María snake, which can attain up to 2m/6ft in length. Remarkable amongst the 1400 molluscs are the snails of the genus Polymita with their colourful marbled houses, typical for the Camagüey province. The most beautiful sight in the animal world is the flamingos on the lagoons of Cayo Coco or Playa Santa Lucía, while the rarest sight is that of feeding manatees and lurking crocodiles in the

FLORA

Typical for Cuba is the *palma real*, the royal palm, which grows up to 40m/130 ft tall. Instead of nuts it has fruit kernels that grow in dense clusters and are used for the extraction of oil. At many beaches you'll see the sturdy sea-grape tree with its hard heart-shaped leaves. Before the arrival of the Spanish, the indigenous people are said to have congregated below the foliage of the sizeable ceiba tree for meetings. The *jagüey* tree, which strangles its host trees to spread its aerial roots, displays bizarre shapes. At higher altitudes pines grow, and many regions were planted with eucalyptus trees to protect the soil from erosion. Amongst the endemic plants are the cork palm, the belly palm and the Cuban pine. Cuba's national flower is the white, very aromatic *mariposa* (butterfly jasmine).

DAVID AGAINST GOLIATH

'Condemn me, it does not matter: you may judge me, history will absolve me.' These words, uttered by Fidel Castro in 1953 during the court case following the failed storming of the Moncada Barracks in Santiago de Cuba, are as topical as ever. Many of Castro's critics have gone quiet since the charismatic patriarch left the stage. What remains, looking back, is half a century of revolutionary achievements unique in Latin America. Two wars of independence

failed on Cuba, the first in the face of Spain's resistance, the second foiled by the intervention of the US. Only the rebels in the Sierra Maestra brought independence, yet also permanent struggle against the US economic embargo: David against Goliath – a fight that isn't yet over, even under Obama as US president. Today though, Cuba can be sure of allies such as Venezuela and Bolivia and enjoys much sympathy worldwide.

LIBRETA

The reason why little is now heard about the *libreta* is that Cubans are now far more interested in consumer goods than worrying about the basic supplies of rice, beans, sugar, milk, eggs or potatoes at prices subsidised by the state. These staple foods are guaranteed to every Cuban citizen by the state, in the shape of the *Libreta de Abastecimiento, Libreta* for short, the 'book of coupons'. Who gets what is regulated by the state according to age and gender. Children under 7 for instance receive a litre of milk a day – as long as there's no scarcity at that particular moment.

LITERATURE

The most important Cuban writers are José Martí (1853–95), José Lezama Lima (1910–76), Alejo Carpentier (1904–80) and the poet Nicolás Guillén (1902–89). The most famous amongst them, at least in Latin America, is José Martí. Affected by political repression early on, he travelled widely and left an extensive oeuvre of letters, speeches, essays and collections of poetry when he died at a young age during the struggle to liberate Cuba. One of the best-known contemporary authors is Miguel Barnet (born 1940), who published 'Cimarrón' (published in English as Biography of a Runaway Slave) in 1966 and opened a cycle on Cuban identity with this story of an escaped slave. The cycle continued with 'A True Story about a Cuban living in New York', and 'Everybody Dreams about Cuba'. Guillermo Cabrera Infante (1929–2005) became well known with his novels 'Three Trapped Tigers' and 'View of Dawn in the Tropics'.

MUSIC

Thanks to Havana's position as a bridgehead between Europe and the New World, Cuba's rhythms, Afro-Spanish with some French influences too, gained great popularity in Europe at an early date, and later in the US as well. Around 1900 this mix resulted in the elegant *danzón* with opulent instrumen-

BOOKS & FILMS

▶ **The Fog of Yesterday** – Thriller by Cuban writer Leonardo Padura, who goes on the trail of an exciting drama from Cuba's revolutionary era

▶ **The Cuban Kitchen** Newly published (2011) illustrated cookbook by Raquel Rabade Roque

▶ **Thine is the Kingdom** – This novel by Cuban author Abilio Estévez depicts Cuba as a place of both paradise and catastrophe

▶ **Buena Vista Social Club** – Globally successful movie (1999) by Wim Wenders and Ry Cooder featuring the legendary vintage stars of Cuban son

▶ **Strawberries and Chocolate** – Wonderful feature film by Cuban star director Tomás Gutiérrez Alea about friendship and tolerance (1993)

▶ **Comandante** – For three days, Oliver Stone chatted to Fidel Castro in 2009 – a portrait that's worth seeing and hearing

Sugar cane is harvested by hand, using a machete

tation. Rural Cubans preferred it lighter and more African, later turning it into the *son* which since Wim Wenders' film 'Buena Vista Social Club' has once again become the musical icon of Cuba. *Trovas* are lovesick troubadour songs accompanied by the guitar, and *nueva trova* their revolutionary political version. Benny Moré, who died at only 43 years of age, is considered the greatest sonero of all times. His compositions influenced the development of salsa. Arguably the most famous Cuban song is 'Guantanamera', with poetic lyrics penned by José Martí.

PARTICULAR

If something is said to be *particular* on Cuba, whether a taxi, a stall or a room for rent, it usually means: this is a private enterprise. The state creams off profits with extremely high taxes – as Cuba is still a communist country.

POPULATION

There are 11.4 million Cubans. At the last census, 65 per cent put their ethnicity down as 'white' (including the Chinese minority), 24.8 per cent as 'mulattoes' and only 0.2 per cent as 'black'. The low percentage of the third category suggests that black skin colour is still seen to be a defect – despite the revolution condemning racism. However, thanks to the revolution there is an awareness of equal rights for everybody at all levels of society. This manifests itself in relatively respectful coexistence and has also kept a certain check on the *machismo* widespread in Latin America.

TOBACCO

Thanks to the island's favourable soil conditions, the world's best tobacco grows in Cuba's western province of Pinar del Río. Following a growth period of three months, the leaves are harvested, sorted and dried. Regular humidification guarantees a consistent fermentation. There are 15 quality categories. The best are the dark leaves *(hojas negras)*. Cigars are made by hand, as you can see if you visit a cigar factory.

FOOD & DRINK

A lime, six fresh mint leaves, a teaspoon of sugar, two centilitres of rum, soda water, garnished with one twig of mint – and you have your Cuban national drink, the *mojito*. Or how about the drink that Ernest Hemingway is said to have loved: a light-green daiquirí from sugar-cane syrup, rum and lime juice?

Or then again maybe you prefer a Mary Pickford, a Havana special, a canchanchara or, last not least, a Cuba libre? Add the ambience of a bar from Havana's famously infamous 1920s and 1930s, when US mafiosi Al Capone and Meyer Lansky were regulars here, most of all though Hemingway, who was not averse to the odd drink or ten. In a way, the cocktail bars still live off the legendary Prohibition era between 1920 and 1933, when

alcohol production and consumption was banned in the US. At the time, Cuba was the only legal fuel stop for drinkers and the hub of alcohol sales, with a tropical location to boot. Hemingway's favourite bar, *El Floridita*, and *La Bodeguita del Medio* are a must when visiting Havana. Whether *Cuba libre*, *mojito* or *daiquirí*: the mixing base is white rum which has matured for five or more years in oak casks. With increasing age it displays a darker colour and is called *añejo*. Rum is enjoyed neat *(ron seco)* or on the rocks *(ron con hielo)*. The world's most famous rum was originally from Cuba: Bacardí. The *Havana Club*, where US businessmen met and the Bacardí distilling dynasty poured rum for its guests, has remained a legend. While

Photo: Boiled lobster

Alongside cocktails, fish and shellfish, Cuban cuisine is enriched by rustic fare using fresh produce from the farmers' markets

the Bacardís fled to Puerto Rico following the revolution, Cuba still looks after the heritage of its most famous family of exiles. The name 'Havana Club' was immortalised in the rum of revolutionary Cuba. While the brand, which is distributed worldwide, is not a serious rival to the Bacardí empire, in terms of quality it matches its pre-revolutionary predecessor. The club in Havana has been restored and reopened as an exclusive meeting place for diplomats and business people. Beer drinkers can choose between sev-

eral brands. A refreshing lager-style beer is *Cristal* for example. Coffee drinkers should try the *café cubano*, which is served black with sugar in small cups. *Guarapo* is the name for cloudy, slightly sweet juice from the sugar cane, refreshing despite its sweetness. A special treat are the freshly squeezed juices of sun-ripened tropical fruit such as *piñas* (pineapple), mangos, papayas, guavas, lemons or limes, oranges and grapefruit. The subject of food was long overshadowed by the difficult supply situation. Oc-

LOCAL SPECIALITIES

▶ **ajiaco bayamés** – stew from Bayamo with pork, maize-flour balls, cumin, tomatoes, onions, garlic, chilli and green bananas

▶ **arroz congrí (oriental)** – rice with beans, garlic and bacon

▶ **arroz con pescado al ron** – rice with fish soaked in rum, spiced with cloves and pepper

▶ **bacalao con plátano** – codfish with cooked green banana

▶ **bocadito** – warm filled bread roll

▶ **calamares** – octopus rings

▶ **carne asada** – seared meat, usually served with carrots, garlic, onions, leek and tomato and spiced with oregano and bay leaf

▶ **coquito blanco** – sweet dessert made from coconut flesh

▶ **parrillada de pescado/carne** – grill platter with various kinds of fish and meat

▶ **patas y panza guisado con arroz blanco** – feet and belly of pork, cooked in water with allspice, salt, concentrated tomato puree and garlic; served with white rice

▶ **pato guisado** – seared duck

▶ **picadillo a la Habanera** – beef mince seared with onions, garlic, tomatoes and wine; it may also be crowned with fried eggs; eaten with white rice

▶ **pollo ahumado** – savoury chicken, smoked before roasting

▶ **pollo frito a la criolla** – chicken pieces marinated in orange, allspice, onions and garlic, and coated in flour before frying

▶ **potaje de frijoles negros** – stew made from black beans with bacon, pieces of chorizo sausage and potatoes, garlic, concentrated tomato puree and onions, spiced with oregano, caraway and salt (photo r.)

▶ **ropa vieja** – 'old clothes', beef cooked to a soft consistency and pulled into pieces, eaten in an aromatic sauce with white rice (photo l.)

casionally you can still feel this. So don't be too surprised when restaurants only have a small selection of dishes or others mentioned on the menu are unavailable 'at the moment'. It's a different situation in the *paladares*, private restaurants. The hosts buy fresh produce at peso prices on the markets and magic them into wonderful Cuban dishes, usually at fair prices. By the way: if guests in a *casa particular* are offered half or full board, this is more than sheer politeness. The hosts

pay high taxes for the right to feed their guests too. If you accept, you'll not only have satisfied your appetite, you'll also have helped your hosts to recoup the tax they paid. However, advise them of your wishes two hours ahead or at breakfast, as some ingredients have still to be got in specially.

One of the most popular dishes is chicken, which the locals like to eat fried nice and crispy. A typical side dish is rice with black beans, *arroz moro.* In soups and as a side dish you'll often see boiled sweet potato *(boniato)*, ñame (yam root) or manioc root *(yuca). Plátanos* (cooking bananas) are often served as fried discs to go with fish or meat.

Soups form an integral part of traditional Cuban cuisine, which has strong Spanish and Moorish influences. You'll often find *sopa de ajo* on the menu, a simple yet delicious garlic soup and originally a Spanish classic.

The major delicacies of course include seafood such as crayfish, which is readily available, at least in the hotels. Fish is served boiled *(hervido)*, fried *(asado)*, oven-baked on pizza and in doughballs, or sometimes as *salpicón* (salad). Do be careful however in state-run restaurants on the motorways or beaches, as some of them get few guests. Like any other restaurant they have a licence to sell crayfish and other seafood, yet due to the scarcity of diners, the creatures are kept in freezers for longer – and on Cuba the electricity supply is as uncertain as the weather during the hurricane season: when the power fails, the content defrosts; when the electricity returns the content freezes again. This does not exactly create salubrious conditions for consumption and it means that crayfish offered illegally, as it were, is not only cheaper but also healthier – even if the hide-and-seek that's often necessary

A feast for the eye: Cuban cocktails

is not everybody's cup of tea. On Cuba, bad stomach bugs are usually down to rotten seafood, and are caused less often by contaminated water. Still, don't forget to ask for *agua sana* (clean water) when ordering drinks with water, and avoid ice cubes and salads.

If you're dining at one of the better restaurants, bear in mind that guests wait at the entrance for the waiter to lead them to a free table. There's usually no need to make a reservation.

SHOPPING

Apart from the classics – cigars, rum or CDs with hot Cuban rhythms – the capital behind the production of many souvenirs in Cuba is the imagination. Improvisation with the materials available has to replace large-scale industrial production. There is certainly no lack of ideas. On the markets, typically Cuban vintage cars manufactured from colourful used drinks cans are amongst the bestsellers. Craft artists outdo each other in the creative use of raw materials such as wood, shells, sisal or fabric, turning them into Creole dolls, garden or children's furniture and jewellery in the most outlandish variations. There is plenty of crochet work, straw hats and bags, reproductions of old Spanish sailing ships in model size. The state, for its part, raided the archives to offer Che Guevara fans the world over likenesses of the glorified revolutionary on t-shirts and postcards, in coffee-table books, on bookends and even on trouser braces.

Usually you can count on the following opening times: shops *Mon–Sat 10/11am–7.30pm*, tourist shops *daily 9am–9pm*, banks/bureaux de change *Mon–Fri 8.30am–noon and 1.30–3pm*, post offices *(correo) Mon–Fri 8am–6pm*.

Shops in the Servi petrol stations are open around the clock.

ART

You'll find a great selection of art from Cuba in Havana, whether in the galleries of the Calle Obispo, in the *Taller experimental de Gráfico* at the Plaza de Catedral or on the art market at the Castillo de la Real Fuerza. You might be able to meet some of the artists in person on the markets. Keep in mind though that works of art and high-end arts and crafts may only be exported up to a value of 1000 US dollars, and you also need a written permit *(autorización)* issued by the *Registro Nacional de Bienes Culturales!*

CIGARS

The best opportunity for buying real Havanas is a visit to one of the many cigar factories *(fábricas de tabaco)*, where you may watch the *tabaqueros* at work. Maybe you'll catch one of the readers who entertaining the workers by reading out stories! Be careful with special offers on the street: they are nearly

Cuba is a great territory for souvenir hunters: art objects, fine Havana cigars, Cuban rum, music for connoisseurs

always fake versions of the globally famous brands such as Cohiba, Romeo y Julieta or Montecristo. Remember that to export more than 23 cigars you need the receipts from the shop in both original and copy (for the customs official); the cigars also have to be in their original packaging and bear the new holographic stamp.

MUSIC

If you want to take home Cuban rhythms, you won't have to look far. Whether in cafés, bars or in a Casa de la Trova: wherever bands play, they'll sell CDs with their music, signed by the artists on request. In terms of audio quality, these CDs are hardly ever first choice. The discs produced at the state-run Egrem studios have much better sound quality and are on offer in any souvenir shop. The selection is particularly good in the ARTEX shops. Musicians currently producing hits

include Adalberto Alvárez, Los Van Van and Manolito. More information on the artists (with online music): *www.egrem. com.cu*

RUM

Rum from the sugar island of Cuba is world-famous for its top quality. Today, Havana Club is the most widely distributed brand of rum on Cuba and the best-known Cuban brand in the world. You can get Havana Club in all hotel shops and souvenir shops. Aged for three years and white, it is the essential high-octane basis for various Cuban cocktails. The wonderfully golden-brown shimmering *Gran Reserva* is matured for several years in specially prepared wooden barrels. Five and seven-year-old Gran Reserva brands are the ones you're most likely to see for sale. They are enjoyed neat or with ice, like a good whisky. *www. havana-club.com*

THE PERFECT ROUTE

START WITH A HISTORY LESSON

① *Holguín* → p. 77 is the gateway to the holiday region in the north of the eponymous province and to the history of Cuba at the same time. Nestling in the hills between **②** *Guardalavaca* → p. 79 and Banes, you'll discover the *Museo de Chorro de Maita* and the *Aldea Taína,* built above the island's largest Indian cemetery. The drive back via *Rafael Freyre* takes you to *Bariay Parque Monumento Nacional* around the historical landing place of Columbus. And on a day trip east to **③** *Birán* → p. 78 you can follow the trail of Fidel and Raúl Castro's youth in the *Finca Mañacas*.

IN THE HEART OF THE ISLAND

Broad pastures, dotted by royal palms, accompany the 440km/275mi drive by car or Viazul bus to the next stop, Trinidad. After 200km/125mi a good opportunity for a break arises in **④** *Camagüey* → p. 63, the 'town of the terracotta jars', which once served to catch rainwater. The pretty colonial *Plaza de San Juan* is a good place to take a break. From Camagüey, another 200km/125mi takes you to **⑤** *Sancti Spíritus* → p. 73 (photo l.), one of the seven oldest cities in Cuba. Narrow alleyways, small squares and a new pedestrian area welcome you to a stroll.

VARIED SOUTHERN COAST

From Sancti Spíritus the Unesco World Heritage town of **⑥** *Trinidad* → p. 72 is only a 45-minute drive away, passing the *Embalse Zaza,* Cuba's largest reservoir lake, as well as the sugar-cane valley of *Valle de los Ingenios (see p. 72)*. If you'd like to go for a dip, head for one of the holiday hotels on the extensive *Playa Ancón (see p. 73)*. Nature lovers should try to find time for a trip to *Topes de Collantes (see p. 73)* (photo r.) in the backcountry of Trinidad, where hiking trails lead to waterfalls. You will see the urban elegance of the 19th and 20th centuries 80km/50mi further west in **⑦** *Cienfuegos* → p. 65, and get glimpses of rural life on the drive via Ariza, Rodas, Yaguaramas, Real Campina and Covadonga to **⑧** *Playa Girón* → p. 61 in the Bay of Pigs. Here, a museum telling the story of the 1961 invasion is worth taking in. Go 40km/25mi further north, always hugging the *Ciénaga de Zapata (see p. 60)*, to La Boca and the **⑨** *Laguna del Tesoro* → p. 60 for a drive into the swamp. After that it's 18km/11mi to the A1 and another 148km/92mi to the country's capital, **⑩** *Havana* → p. 32.

Experience the many facets of Cuba from east to west and back again, with short detours to the left and right of the main route

EAST OF HAVANA

Havana's city beaches, the *Playas del Este (see p. 48)*, are reached via the tunnel and the signposted turn-off onto the fast *Vía Blanca* road. A good view of the spectacular *Bacunayagua* bridge spanning the Yumurí Valley can be had from the *Mirador del Yumurí*. After that, the road descends in bends down to the bay of ⑪ *Matanzas* → p. 61. After crossing Río Canimar you reach ⑫ *Varadero* → p. 55. The peninsula with its endless beaches is the island's oldest tourist centre. Step back into vibrant Cuban life in nearby *Cárdenas (see p. 60),* where horse-drawn carriages are still used to get around.

PLANTATIONS, HISTORY, BEACHES

The exit signposted Máximo Gómez leads past neglected sugar-cane fields to the Colón turn. Plantations with tropical fruit now dominate the scenery – at least up to Che Guevara's town: ⑬ *Santa Clara* → p. 70. In the northeast the colonial beauty of ⑭ *Remedios* → p. 71 and the offshore *Cayos Las Brujas* and *Santa María* with pretty beaches are worth stopping for. Driving across the sea on a causeway has got to be one of the most beautiful experiences on Cuba. A good two-hour drive further on, via ⑮ *Morón* → p. 70, you are treated to the same experience, this time with flamingos that breed in their thousands in the ⑯ *Jardines del Rey* → p. 68. This marks the end of the perfect route; return to Holguín via Ciego de Ávila on the Autopista.

1780km/1100mi. Driving time only: approx. 26 hours. Recommended trip duration: 10 days. Detailed map of the route in the road atlas, the pull-out map and on the back cover

HAVANA

MAP IN THE BACK COVER
(121 E–F2) *(ⅢD2)* **'In Havana, my friend, anything goes, as long as you're not a bore.' This is what folk wisdom has to say about life in Cuba's capital city.**

This assessment was never so timely as now, as a variety of small businesses show the slow-moving socialist state enterprises what is possible – and this despite high taxation. Today, the streets are lined with small snack stalls selling hamburgers, hotdogs, pizza or fresh fruit juices; bike rickshaws offer their services as well as private taxis – and all this in Cuban peso prices for Cubans and at the correct rate of exchange in CUC. Not that the bureaux de change have disappeared. One system works alongside the

other; the whole thing seems a bit like a secret takeover of Havana by its citizens and free enterprise. The encouraging framework for this was created by city historian Eusebio Leal with his grand-scale restoration of the Old Town. This is far from being completed. It did however create a new Havana, which doesn't destroy itself anymore, a city that can be a player on the global stage again, in short a city that is in love with itself again after a long revolution-induced break. Little matter that the side streets of the Centro, for instance, still feature a number of towering scrap heaps and that crumbling façades of houses still bear witness to past disdain.

The biggest attraction of Havana (pop. 3 million) is the historic Old Town, which

---

Photo: Vintage car in front of the Capitol in Havana

Bars, bodegas and bastion walls: no other Caribbean city charms visitors in the same way as the Unesco World Heritage city of Havana

in 1982 was given World Heritage status by Unesco. Typical for *Habana vieja* are narrow street canyons cutting through high baroque and neo-classical buildings. Stroll across squares with ancient cobbles where once the carriages of the fine folk used to park, past high double doors offering glimpses of aristocratic entrance halls or column-framed *patios*, step onto marble floors and run your hand over curved mahogany balustrades. The famous ● *Malecón* too, begins in the Old Town: turned longingly, you could say, to-

wards the Straits of Florida, it is the quay wall of the *enamorados*, lovers, and a show boulevard lined with columned façades, some of which have now been restored. Curving for miles along the coast towards the west, past the quarters of the Centro and the more recent Vedado, the Malecón ends at the tunnel to Quinta Avenida, the prestigious villa-lined street of Miramar, where many embassies are based. And in the east where the boulevard turns into Avenida del Puerto, you can branch off into the tunnel running

On a Sunday, Callejón del Hamel has dance and music

under the narrowest point of the harbour entrance. The tunnel leads into the Vía Monumental with its access road to the Complejo El Morro. The Vía Monumental then takes you to the Vía Blanca, whose exits fork off to the pretty beaches of the Playas del Este, and which then leads on to Varadero.

HABANA VIEJA/CENTRO

★ Alley after alley, square after square adorned with magnificent buildings from various eras – and music everywhere: Habana vieja, the Old Town, is a vibrant monument to the centuries-long, almost uninterrupted rise of the city which was once one of the wealthiest in the Americas.

Every era left its trace. The parts of the Old Town still dating back to its founding period in the mid-16th century – when Spain elevated the small Villa San Cristóbal de La Habana founded by Diego Velázquez to the status of *Puerto Principal* – are the Plaza de Armas, the Fort Castillo

WHERE TO START?
Parque Central (U E2–3) *(𝄞 e2–3):* This square is an international meeting place and tourist interface. In front of the *Hotel Parque Central* you'll find ● vintage taxis (Chrysler Bel Air) waiting to take you on a tour of the city for 20 CUC/hr; the stop for the good-value hop-on-hop-off sightseeing buses of Habana Bus Tour is in front of the *Hotel Inglaterra*, and if you need to book trips or rental cars, head for the arcade at nearby *Hotel Sevilla*. From Parque Central, it's only a few paces to the Old Town, the Prado and the Malecón.

de Real Fuerza and the streets of Los Oficios and Los Mercaderes. The reason for this promotion to a harbour where all Spanish treasure ships from Central and South America gathered is still evident: the aim was to defend vast riches against pirates, as shown by remains of the old city wall, a few scattered defensive walls or baluartes, and most of all the gigantic fortified complex of Morro-Cabaña.

Everywhere you go, you'll meet signs of Cuba's former status as the world's biggest sugar producer: splendid aristocratic palaces with long wooden balconies, baronial portals or high wooden doors with imaginative *aldabas* (door knockers), leading on to arcaded patios and into rooms with precious coffered ceilings. They are a reminder of the fabled wealth of the people who were sent from Spain to govern the colony. Bordering the Old Town to the south is the *Cerro* quarter with the last of the 19th-century *quintas* (summer houses). At the Parque Central, the capitol and the old *Barrio Chino* we have already come to Habana Centro. In Calle Galiano and Calle Rafael the quarter has its own shopping streets, and at the Malecón it looks its best: with neo-classical or art deco façades and high-ceilinged colonnades.

SIGHTSEEING

INSIDER TIP ▶ CALLEJÓN DE HAMEL ●
(U B–C2) (*ⴔ b–c2*)
Worth a visit for the wall paintings in the alleyway, the small Santería shop stuffed full of cult objects, and the corner café. Traditionally, most Sundays at noon, a lively street party takes place (sadly, irregularly these days): bands drum for all they're worth, and Cubans dance themselves into a trance right there on the street. *Hamel | betw. Aramburu/Hospital*

CALLE OBISPO
(U E–F2) (*ⴔ e–f2*)
Take a stroll on this pleasant boulevard with cafés, restaurants and shops of all kinds. It crosses Havana's Old Town from the Parque Central to the Plaza de Armas. Once the main commercial artery, Calle Obispo as the seat of the National Bank (1907) is the 'Wall Street' of Havana. Don't miss a visit to the old *Taquechel pharmacy (no. 155)*, faithfully restored to its former glory. In the *Ambos Mundos* hotel *(52 rooms | tel. 07 8 60 95 30 | www.hotelambosmundos-cuba.com | Moderate)* on the corner of Calle Mercaderes you can visit INSIDER TIP ▶ Ernest Hemingway's former room.

★ **Habana vieja**
The Old Town: old alleyways taking on a new shine
→ p. 34

★ **Quinta Avenida**
Street of splendour in the embassy quarter → p. 43

★ **Cabaret Tropicana**
This world-famous dance revue is a must → p. 46

★ **Nacional de Cuba**
Hotel with a notorious past
→ p. 47

★ **Playas del Este**
Magnificent beaches near the capital → p. 48

★ **Museo Hemingway**
The winner of the Nobel Prize for Literature lived and worked here → p. 48

MARCO POLO HIGHLIGHTS

CASA DE ÁFRICA (U F2) (*m f2*)

What you can see here, alongside 'souvenirs' that Fidel Castro brought back from trips to Africa, are cult objects used by Afro-Cuban priests during their ceremonies. *Calle Obrapia 157 | betw. Mercaderes/San Ignacio | Tue–Sat 9.30am–5pm, Sun 9.30am–12.30pm | admission 2 CUC*

A monument of defence: the Castillo del Moro

COMPLEJO EL MORRO-CABAÑA ⚲ (U E–F1) (*m e–f1*)

Begun in 1589, the *Castillo de los Tres Reyes del Morro (daily 10am–6pm | admission 2 CUC)* forms the older part of the fortified complex. The master builder involved was the Italian Battista Antonelli, who was also behind the defensive system of Cartagena (Colombia). Next door, the large *Fortaleza de la Cabaña (daily 10am–4pm | admission 4 CUC)* was established following the withdrawal of the English in 1764. Behind its fine gateway lies an impressive complex, boasting a weapons museum *(Museo de Armas y Fortificaciones)*, the old headquarters of Che Guevara *(Museo Memorial Comandancia del Che)*, a cafeteria and a few souvenir shops. *Access from the Old Town through the tunnel; daily 9am–10pm | admission to the complex without visiting the fort 1 CUC.* If you want to visit during the traditional ceremony of the *cañonazo* (firing of the cannons, *daily 9pm*), entrance to the complex costs 6 CUC.

MAQUETA DE LA HABANA VIEJA (U F2) (*m f2*)

The Old Town with 3500 buildings is reproduced here in exact detail in a small format, to a scale of 1:500. If you like, you can watch a film on Habana vieja here too. *Mercaderes 116 | betw. Obispo/Obrapía | daily 9am–6.30pm | admission 1, photo permit 2, video permit 5 CUC*

MUSEO DEL AUTOMÓVIL ● (U F2) (*m f2*)

A treat not just for car lovers: the oldest amongst the 45 vintage cars is a 1905 Cadillac. *Oficios no. 13 | betw. Justiz/Obrapia | Tue–Sat 9am–5pm, Sun 9am–1pm | admission 1, photo permit 2, video 10 CUC (per camera)*

MUSEO RON HAVANA CLUB (U E2) (*m e2*)

This museum is all about rum and does a good job of showing all steps of the production process – fermentation, distilling, filtering and maturating – using tools, equipment and containers.

The star of the show here is the 1930 INSIDER TIP ▶ model of a sugar factory, the *Central Azucarero La Esperanza*. When the transport trains are put to work, sound effects come on, and there is even a fire glowing in the oven. Part of the Fundación set-up are a shop and a reconstruction of the legendary *Sloppy Joe* bar, where island VIPs used to meet in the 1940s. *Ave. del Puerto No. 262/ corner Calle Sol | daily 9am–15.30pm | 7 CUC incl. guided tour | www.havanaclub foundation.com*

MUSEO NACIONAL DE BELLAS ARTES
(U E2) (*ऻ e2*)

The national museum of the fine arts is housed in two separate buildings: gems of Cuban painting from different centuries can be found in the modern building on Calle Trocadero *(betw. Zulueta/Montserrate)*, while the collection of international art is housed in the former *Centro Asturiano* on Calle San Rafael *(betw. Zulueta/Montserrate)*, which was built in 1928 taking the Paris Opera as its model. *Both Tue–Sat 10am–6pm, Sun 10am–2pm | combined ticket 8, individually 5 CUC each | www.museonacional.cult.cu*

MUSEO DE LA REVOLUCIÓN ●
(U E2) (*ऻ e2*)

The most comprehensive of the country's many museums dedicated to the revolution is housed in three storeys of the former Presidential Palace (1920). This is also where you can admire the famous life-size figures of Che Guevara and Camilo Cienfuegos, represented in guerrilla action. The showpiece is the 11 × 30m/36 x 100ft Hall of Mirrors. In front of the museum, the *Garita de la Maestranza* is a reminder of the course of the old wall. The museum gardens hold the *Memorial Granma* (access via the museum), a huge display case with the eponymous yacht

used by the 1956 rebels to land on Cuba. *Ave. de las Misiones | betw. Monserrate and Zulueta | daily 10am–5pm | admission 6 CUC, guided tour additional 2 CUC*

PARQUE CENTRAL/PRADO
(U E2–3) (*ऻ e2–3*)

Magnificent square on the border between Havana vieja and Centro, which along with *Paseo de Martí (Prado)* illustrates Havana's wealth at the start of the 20th century. Nearby, you can't miss the *National Capitol* (currently closed for renovation works), the former House of Representatives (1929) inspired by the Capitol in Washington. Diagonally across, friends of Santería will find the *Museo de los Orishas (Paseo del Prado 615 | betw. Monte/Dragones | daily 9am–5pm | admis-*

Camilo Cienfuegos and Che Guevara
in the Museo de la Revolución

sion 10, from 2 people 6 CUC each). Next to the Capitol, on the right, it's hard to ignore the over-laden eclectic façade of the former *Centro Gallego* (early 20th century); its right half houses the *Gran Teatro* with the *García Lorca* hall, seat of the

PLAZA DE ARMAS (U F2) (ɯ f2)

This secluded square with a famous ceiba tree is dominated by the *Palacio de los Capitanes Generales*, the former governmental and residential seat of the captains general, built in 1791. Today,

The squat cathedral dominates the Plaza de la Catedral

Cuban National Ballet *(tel. 07 8 62 94 73)*. A few steps further on, the longest-established hotel in town, the *Inglaterra (83 rooms | tel. 07 8 60 85 93, 07 8 60 85 97 | www.gran-caribe.com | Moderate)*, with its grand salons and modernised rooms, is the accommodation of choice for nostalgic holidaymakers.

Opposite you'll find the classical *Edificio Manzana de Gomez Mena*, built in 1917. Behind, in Calle Montserrate, rises the former headquarters of the pre-revolutionary Bacardí rum dynasty, the *Edificio Bacardí* (1930), a masterpiece of art deco. Today, European travel agencies have opened their Havana offices here.

the palace houses the *city museum* with its 25 exhibition rooms, some of which feature fine furniture from the 18th and 19th centuries *(daily 10am–6pm | admission 3 CUC)*. At the opposite end of the square, the former palace of the Duke of Santovenia is now occupied by the small and classy *Santa Isabel* hotel *(27 rooms | tel. 07 8 60 82 01 | Expensive)*. Occupying a large swathe of space between them, a pretty INSIDER TIP market for antiquarian books *(Mon–Sat 9am–6pm)* will particularly appeal to book lovers with a good level of Spanish. Towards the north *(Calle O'Reilly)*, the square is flanked by the oldest preserved fortress in Havana, the *Castillo de la Real Fuerza*

(1558–77). Watching processes from atop the tower is one of the splendid emblems of Havana: *La Giraldilla.* The bronze statue represents noblewoman Inés de Bobadilla waiting in vain for her husband, the Spanish governor Hernando de Soto, who lost his life in 1542 on the Mississippi. Inside, a display of Cuban ceramics awaits *(Tue–Sat 9.30am–5pm, Sun 9.30am–1pm).*

PLAZA DE LA CATEDRAL (U F2) (𝄢 f2)

Havana's most beautiful historic square is dominated by the baroque shell-limestone façade of the *cathedral.* Begun in 1748 by the Jesuits – who would later be chased from the island – the church was completed in 1789 by the Spanish colonial government. The frescoes and the main altar were created by the Italian artists Bianchini and Peruvani. Opposite the cathedral, the former *Palace of the Count of Bayona* (1720) shelters the *Museo de Arte Colonial,* which shows precious exhibits from the colonial period *(Tue–Sun 9.30am–5pm / admission 2 CUC).* Adorned with pretty arcades, the building housing the trendy *El Patio* restaurant used to be the palace of the Counts of Aguas Claras; the restaurant serves good Creole food, e.g. *pierna de cerdo al jugo,* juicy pork chop *(tel. 07 8 67 10 35 / daily noon–11pm, bar open round the clock / Moderate).* Art lovers will be interested in the *Centro de Arte Contemporáneo Wifredo Lam (Calle San Ignacio / corner of Empedrado / Mon–Sat 10am–5pm / admission 2 CUC)* on the left-hand side of the cathedral, which in spring 2013 hosts the 12th biennial of Havana *(www.bienalhabana.cult.cu).* The arts centre is named after the Cuban artist Wifredo Lam (1902–82), who studied art in Madrid, was in contact with the Surrealists in Paris and also lived in New York for a while.

PLAZA DE SAN FRANCISCO (U F4) (𝄢 f4)

Completely restored, including its lion fountain, this square is situated opposite the cruise terminal. Here you'll find the Chamber of Commerce *(Lonja del Comercio,* and the San Francisco monastery, today the only sacred art museum of Havana *(Museo de Arte Religioso / Mon–Sat 9am–5pm / admission 2 CUC),* as well as popular eateries. The *Café del Oriente* gourmet restaurant *(tel. 07 8 60 66 86 / restaurant daily noon–midnight / Expensive)* is worth a visit.

PLAZA VIEJA/CONVENTO DE SANTA CLARA (U F3) (𝄢 f3)

This is the only square in Old Havana that wasn't laid out together with a church, a fortress or governmental building. The most imposing house,

LOW BUDGET

▶ A comfortable and cheap way to get around Havana's Old Town are the *bici-taxis* (bike rickshaws). A trip will only set you back around 2–3 CUC.

▶ Sightseeing as much as you like for 5 CUC a day: hop-on-hop-off buses ply three routes, that may be combined too: Old Town, Playas del Este (departure across from Hotel *Inglaterra*), as well as Miramar (departure from Plaza de la Revolución/same stop as Old Town bus).

▶ ● A carriage ride through the Old Town doesn't have to be expensive if you share the fun and price (20 CUC) with friends or other tourists. Lean back and enjoy the two-horsepower trip (leaving from Parque Central).

adorned with a cast-iron balcony, is the *Casa del Conde de Jaruco* (1768). The *Gómez Vila* (1909) at the corner houses the **INSIDER TIP** *Cámera oscura (daily 9am–6pm | admission 2 CUC)*, which gives an overview of the surroundings in real-time projection. Diagonally opposite, the *Taberna La Muralla (corner of Calle La Muralla | daily Budget–Moderate)* draws in the crowds. Spreading on nearby Calle Cuba no. 610 (betw. Calle Sol/Luz), the former *Convento de Santa Clara*, founded in 1638, used to be the oldest convent in Havana; today, it's the seat of the city department for the conservation of monuments *(visits Mon–Fri 9am–4pm | admission 2 CUC)*.

CITY WALL/MUSEO CASA NATAL DE JOSÉ MARTÍ (U F4) *(ⓜ f4)*
The biggest remaining chunk of the city wall can be seen next to the main station (1912). Opposite the railway station, the birthplace of José Martí holds a museum dedicated to the life of the freedom hero and poet *(C. Leonor Pérez 314 | Tue–Sat 9am–5pm, Sun 9am–12.45pm | admission 2 CUC)*.

FOOD & DRINK

CASTILLO DE FARNÉS (UE2) *(ⓜ e2)*
The waiter will be happy to show you the table where Fidel Castro, his brother Raúl, and Che Guevara had a meal on 9 January 1959. A photograph documents the event. The food is good and good-value too. *Monserrate 401 | corner Obrapía | tel. 07 8 67 10 30 | daily noon–midnight | Moderate*

INSIDER TIP LA GUARIDA (UC2) *(ⓜ c2)*
Since parts of the 1994 film Fresa y chocolate (Strawberry and Chocolate) were filmed here. This *paladar* is often fully booked, so ring ahead to reserve a table! *Calle Concordia 418 | betw. Gervasio/Es-cobar, 3rd floor | tel. 07 8 66 90 47 | daily noon–4pm, 7pm–midnight | Expensive*

HANOI (U E3) *(ⓜ e3)*
Nothing Vietnamese, but rather typically Cuban fare is served in this well-kept corner restaurant with garden, e.g. *ropa vieja* ('old clothing', meat braised with chickpeas and tomatoes) and other Creole dishes, all tasty and at fair prices. *Calle Teniente Rey, corner Bernaza | tel. 07 8 67 10 29 | daily 11.45am–midnight | Budget*

MESÓN DE LA FLOTA (U F3) *(ⓜ f3)*
Restaurant in the style of a Spanish tavern, offering appetising Spanish fare. A big draw are the **INSIDER TIP** flamenco shows every evening at 8.30pm. *Calle Mercaderes betw. Teniente Rey/Amargura | tel. 07 8 63 38 38 | daily from 1pm | Budget–Moderate*

LOS NARDOS (U E3) *(ⓜ e3)*
Artists and intellectuals meet in the restaurant of the Sociedad Juventud Asturiana. Generous portions, acceptable prices. *Paseo del Prado 563 | on 1st floor | tel. 07 8 63 29 85 | daily noon–midnight | Moderate–Expensive*

PASTELERÍA FRANCESA (U E2–3) *(ⓜ e2–3)*
This well-stocked French bakery, which also serves sandwiches, is currently a favourite haunt of both residents and tourists. *Prado 410 (next to Hotel Inglaterra) | tel. 8 62 07 39 | daily 8am–midnight | Budget*

LA TERRAZA (U E2) *(ⓜ e2)*
Gourmet restaurant in the building belonging to the *Federación de Asociaciones Asturianas* opened in 2010. For fine views across the Prado, try the *Oviedo* bar in the upper floor. *Prado 309, corner of Virtudes | tel. 07 862326 | daily noon–midnight | Moderate–Expensive*

LA ZARAGOZANA (U E3) *(⊞ e3)*
While Havana's oldest restaurant (founded in 1830) serves a fine filet mignon, the pièce de résistance here is the paella zaragozana. *Montserrate | betw. Obispo/Obrapia | tel. 07 8 671 0 40 | daily noon–midnight | Expensive*

SHOPPING

LA FERIA DE LOS ARTESANOS ●
(U F4) *(⊞ f4)*
Artists of all styles exhibit their works in former warehouses. In amongst a lot of kitsch, those in the know may well discover some bargains (don't forget to get a confirmation with export permit stamp!). *Centro Cultural Antiguos Almacenes de Depósito San José | daily 10am–6pm*

GALERÍA MANOS (U E 2–3) *(⊞ e2–3)*
This shop promoting the work of Cuban craftspeople is the best address for discerning souvenir hunters. *Obispo 411 (next to the souvenir market)*

INSIDER TIP ▶ MUSEO DEL CHOCOLATE
(U F3) *(⊞ f3)*
Delicious pralines are produced here right in front of visitors and shoppers. The chocolate comes from Baracoa. A display case shows antique cocoa cups and ingredients for making chocolate. *Mercaderes 255 | corner Amargura*

QUITRÍN (U E2) *(⊞ e2)*
Chic white cotton fashion, inspired by Cuban folklore. *Obispo 153 | corner San Ignacio*

CIGAR FACTORY PARTAGÁS ●
(U E3) *(⊞ e3)*
Naturally, the longest-established cigar factory (in business since 1845) may not only be visited but also features a small shopping paradise for cigar lovers. *Calle Industría 520 | behind the Capitol | factory visits Mon–Fri 9.30–11am and 12.30–3pm | price 10 CUC*

ENTERTAINMENT

LA BODEGUITA DEL MEDIO ●
(U F2) *(⊞ f2)*
Mostly tourists crowd this super-cosy bar to taste the famous house speciality, the rum-mint-lime *mojito* cocktail. *Empedrado 207 | tel. 07 8 671 3 74 | daily noon–0.45am*

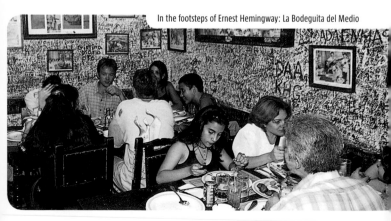
In the footsteps of Ernest Hemingway: La Bodeguita del Medio

CAFÉ PARIS (U F2) (*m f2*)
Popular wooden-panelled corner bar, usually with live music in the evenings. *Obispo 202/San Ignacio | tel. 07 8 62 04 66 | daily 24-hour | Budget*

EL FLORIDITA (U E3) (*m e3*)
The cradle of the *daiquirí* cocktail. 'Papa Hemingway' was a regular here, and the management has immortalised him in his favourite corner with a bronze sculpture. The restaurant is particularly good for crayfish and fish. *Obispo 557 | corner Monserrate | tel. 07 8 67 13 00 | daily noon–10pm, bar to midnight | Moderate–Expensive*

WHERE TO STAY

CASA COLONIAL CARY Y NILO
(U C2) (*m c2*)
Quiet and safe *casa particular* (private residence) near the paladar of *La Guari-*da. 2 air-conditioned en-suite rooms | *Gervasio 216 | betw. Concordia/Virtudes | tel. 07 8 62 71 09 | orixl@yahoo.es, caridadgf45@yahoo.es | Budget*

CASA ROLANDO ☆ (U D2) (*m d2*)
Residing on the 5th floor of a highrise in Centro with two private rooms gives you a great view from the balcony. *Calle Aguila 314 | tel. 07 8 67 74 71 | www.casarolando.com | Budget*

DEAUVILLE (U D2) (*m d2*)
Since the food and service have improved, this highrise has regained its status as one of the recommended hotels; its location on the Malecón has always been top. Fantastic views from the ☆ top seaview rooms; there's also a pool and in-house club. *144 rooms | Av. de Italia 1/San Lázaro | tel. 07 8 66 88 12 | Moderate*

Pool on the roof and a view across the city: Hotel Deauville

FLORIDA (U F2) (*m f2*)
The best choice for those who like to be housed right at the heart of things. On the pretty patio you'll feel like you've travelled back in time. From 10pm onwards, the smoky INSIDER**TIP** *Magato* piano bar becomes a rendezvous for good salsa dancers *(admission 10 CUC).* *25 rooms | Calle Obispo 252/Cuba | tel. 07 8 62 41 27 | www.habaguanexhotels.com | Expensive*

LOS FRAILES (U F3) (*m f3*)
While staff are not recruited from real monks, they do go about their tasks in decorative monk's cowls. In this hostal housed in an 18th-century palacio the real world recedes quite quickly. *22 rooms | Calle Teniente Rey 8 | betw. Oficios/Mercaderes | tel. 07 8 62 93 83 | www.hotellosfrailescuba.com | Moderate–Expensive*

PARQUE CENTRAL (U E3) (*₥ e3*)
There's a fair bit of luxury hiding behind
the remaining façade of a 17th-century
palace; the house has a central location
and offers all mod cons. In the lobby,
even non-residents can use free Wi-Fi.
*279 rooms | Calle Neptuno | betw. Paseo
del Prado/Zulueta | tel. 07 8 60 66 27 |
www.hotelparquecentral.com | Expensive*

RAQUEL (U F3) (*₥ f3*)
Grandiose art nouveau hotel with Jew-
ish origins, famous for its stained-glass
dome and the good views from the
● roof terrace, one of the most beautiful chill-out spaces in the entire Old
Town. Spacious rooms. *25 rooms | Calle
Amargura 103 | corner San Ignacio | www.
hotelraquel-cuba.com | Moderate*

SARATOGA (U E3) (*₥ e3*)
The legendary hotel from the wild 1930s
is open for business again. *89 rooms, 7
suites | Paseo del Prado Nr. 603/Dragones |
tel. 07 8 68 10 00 (ext. 4400) | www.hotel-
saratoga.com | Expensive*

SEVILLA (U E2) (*₥ e2*)
A gem from the early 20th century; the
elegant ☼ rooftop garden yields fine
views of the Old Town. In the arcade
around the corner (access from the hotel
is usually locked) you'll find all important Cuban travel agencies and car hire
representations. *181 rooms | Trocadero
55 | betw. Paseo de Martí/Zulueta | tel.
07 8 60 85 60 | www.hotelsevillacuba.
com | Expensive*

HOSTAL VALENCIA (U F3) (*₥ f3*)
This friendly little guesthouse with its
cosy courtyard has only 12 rooms, all
however equipped with air-conditioning
and bathroom. *Calle Oficios 53/Obrapía |
tel. 07 8 67 10 37 | www.habaguanex
hotels.com | Moderate*

INFORMATION

INFOTUR (U E2) (*₥ e2*)
State-run tourist information office:
*Obispo (betw. Bernaza/Villegas) | tel. 07
33 33 33, 07 8 62 45 86; Obispo/San Igna-
cio | tel. 07 8 63 68 84 | www.infotur.cu*

TRIPS

CUBA REAL TOURS (U E2) (*₥ e2*)
Travelling around Cuba as an independent traveller? The office of this tour operator has ideas for rental-car tours and tips.
Longer trips with an indi-
vidual touch are on offer too.
*Calle Montserrate 261 | corner San Juan
de Dios | Edificio Barcadí, Oficina 404 |
tel. 07 8 66 42 51 | www.cubarealtours.eu*

MIRAMAR/ VEDADO

(U A1–3) (*₥ a1–3*) **Vedado's main artery of La Rampa ends where the Hotel
Nacional rises on a rocky outcrop.**
This quarter was built in the mid-19th
century according to modern ideas of
urban planning, when main streets such
as Línea und Calzada and broad boule-
vards such as the Avenida de los Presi-
dentes and Paseo were laid out. The latter leads to the Plaza de la Revolución.
On Calle L, on a hill, you'll find the main
entrance to the University of Havana,
'La Colina' for short. During the prohibition era in the US, when the centre of
Vedado turned into a sin strip of bars,
the wealthy moved further west, to *Miramar*. This quarter begins where the
Malecón ends. Its main artery is the
most glorious street in the Caribbean,
★ *Quinta Avenida*. Quinta Avenida
leads into the world of the top embas-

sies and company headquarters, as well as the aristocratic homes of noble families, new luxury hotels, and last not least, to Marina Hemingway, Cuba's largest.

SIGHTSEEING

CEMENTERIO COLÓN

You stroll (or drive) across this impressive cemetery as you would through a noble quarter of the palaces of the dead. Amongst over 53,000 tombs look out for the ones of Che photographer Alberto 'Korda' Gutierrez, writer Alejo Carpentier and Buena Vista Social Club star Ibrahim Ferrer (1927–2005), amongst others. The oldest part of the cemetery, used until 1875, is the subterranean *Galería de Tobías*, which was inaugurated by the architect of the cemetery, Calixto de Loira, a year after it was founded. *Main entrance: Zapata and Calle 12 | daily 8am–5pm | admission 5 CUC*

MAQUETA DE LA HABANA COLOSAL MINIATURA

Havana on a 1:1000 scale. Architect Mario Coyula used mostly cedar wood for the 22 × 8m/72 x 26ft model of the city. *Calle 28 no. 113 | betw. 1/3 | Tue–Sat 9.30am–5pm | admission 3, photo/video permits 2/5 CUC*

MUSEO COMPAY SEGUNDO

In the house where Compay Segundo (1907–2003) lived, photographs and documents tell of the life of the Buena Vista Social Club star musician. *Calle 22, no. 103 | corner 1ra/3ra | Mon–Fri 10am–noon, 2–4pm (telephone reservations: 07 20 6 86 29) | free admission*

MUSEO DE LA DANZA

The Museum of Dance is a homage to the iconic ballerina Alicia Alonso, director of the Cuban national ballet and friend of Fidel Castro's. On view are paintings, stage dresses, dancing shoes and photos of famous dancers. *Línea*

Even death is given a dramatic stage setting: tombs on the Cementerio Colón

365/G | Tue–Sat 11am–6.30pm | admission 2 CUC

MUSEO NACIONAL DE ARTES DECORATIVAS

Outside and inside, Cuba's most opulent example of noble living in pre-revolutionary times: built in the 1920s for María Gómez Mena, Countess of Revilia de Camargo, the villa shelters precious exhibits, including Sèvres porcelain, Chippendale furniture and silver work by Paul de Lamerie. The palace is framed by a well-planned garden: to the right, flowers blossom according to the different seasons, to the left the 'night' garden brings coolness. *Calle 17, no. 502 | betw. D and E | Tue–Sat 10.30am–5.45pm, Sun 9am–1pm | admission 3 CUC*

FOOD & DRINK

EL ALJIBE

Large terrace restaurant next to the *Dos Gardenias*. The speciality here is *pollo* (chicken). *Miramar | 7a Ave. | betw. Calle 24 and 26 | tel. 07 2 04 15 83 | daily noon–midnight | Budget–Moderate*

INSIDER TIP ATELIER

Paladar where you dine as if in an art gallery for young Cuban artists. The food is also creative, as evidenced by starters such as salmon rolls with cheese or *malangitas* with a honey dip (malanga is a kind of Caribbean cabbage which is finely grated, mixed with egg and deep-fried). *Calle 5ta no. 511 altos | betw. Paseo and Calle 2 | tel. 07 8 36 20 25 | daily noon–midnight | Moderate*

EL EMPERADOR (U A2) (🗺 a2)

Havana lies at your feet here: this restaurant (good international cooking) on the 33rd floor crowns the *Edificio FOCSA* building – the city's highest, which can be seen from afar. The seats next to the windows, going right down to the floor, are only recommended for those immune to vertigo. *Calle 17 | betw. M and N | daily noon–2pm | Moderate*

HELADERÍA COPPELIA (U A2) (🗺 a2)

Famous through the Fresa y chocolate film, this ice-cream palace of 1966 continues to be a popular meeting place for the sweet-toothed brigade on the La Rampa/Calle L. crossroads. *Vedado | Tue–Sun 11am–10.30pm*

PALADAR ESPERANZA

It's all nice and fluffy here, cosy and just plain tasty. The recipes here have been handed down the family (do reserve a table!). *Miramar | Calle 16 no. 105 | betw. 1/3 | tel. 07 2 02 43 61 | Fri/Sat 7–11pm | Expensive*

EL TOCORORO

This exclusive seafood restaurant has seen its fair share of VIP diners. One salon is reserved for sushi lovers. *Miramar | Calle 18/Ave. 3ra | tel. 07 2 04 22 09 | Mon–Sat noon–midnight | Moderate*

1830/JARDINES 1830 (U B1) (🗺 b1)

Popular for weddings, the elegant *1830* restaurant forms a unit with the partly Japanese-inspired *Jardines 1830* garden restaurant behind. Don't miss the open-air INSIDER TIP salsa matinée every Sunday between 5 and 10pm, when passionate salsa dancers meet right by the sea. *Malecón 1252/Calle 20 | tel. 07 8 38 30 90 (-92) | daily noon–midnight | Budget– Expensive*

SPORTS & ACTIVITIES

CLUB HAVANA ●

Now also accessible for tourists, the former *Biltmore* yacht club and today's dip-

lomats' club is an exclusive spa spot: gym, private beach, pool, sauna, jacuzzi, humidor, restaurant. *Ave. 5ta | betw. 188 and 92 | tel. 07 2 04 57 00 | admission 20 CUC (incl. food & drink coupon worth 10 CUC)*

MARINA HEMINGWAY

Cuba's largest marina is equipped with everything the sailor needs: restaurants,

with 200,000 visitors. *Calle 72 no. 4504 | betw. 41 and 45 | tel. 07 2 67 17 17 | daily from 8pm, show from 10pm | admission from 70 CUC (incl. drinks and snacks)*

CAFÉ CANTANTE (U A4) (🛱 a4)

The best live salsa bands take the dance floor to boiling point. Cellar bar near the Teatro Nacional. *Calle Paseo/C. 39 | Plaza*

Opulent glamour show for tourists: Cabaret Tropicana

shops, hotels. Diving and snorkelling trips can be arranged here. *5ta Ave./248 | tel. 07 2 04 50 88 | www.nauticamarlin.com*

ENTERTAINMENT

CABARET TROPICANA ★ ●

World-famous dance revue in glitzy costumes; this is where the best revue girls in Cuba take to the stage. An extravaganza beyond compare of Latin American dances and rhythms awaits you! This revue theatre was founded in 1939 (with a casino attached at the time) by Cuban artist Victor de Correa. In the 70th jubilee year, director David Varela celebrated record-breaking attendances

de la Revolución | tel. 07 8 78 42 73 | daily 11.30pm–4am | admission from 10 CUC

CASA DE LA MÚSICA

Concerts in the house of the Egrem music studios; the attached shop is a must for aficionados of Cuban music. *Calle 20 no. 3308/Calle 35 | tel. 07 2 04 04 47 | 5pm–9pm (disco 11pm–4am)*

INSIDER TIP ▶ DON CANGREJO

By day, in its incarnation as a fish restaurant, this place leads a fairly modest existence. In the evenings however, half of Havana congregates here – artists, students and other intellectuals – to listen to live concerts by Cuban Fusion, In-

teractivo, Kelvis Ochoa, Decemer Bueno or Raul Paz. Super ambience under the stars, with pool and right by the sea. *Av. 1ra | betw. 16 and 18 | tel. 07 2 04 50 02*

LA MAISON

Elegant address for fashion victims; INSIDER**TIP** shows from 10pm in the pool garden, followed by dancing at club *Temba* (for the over-30s). *Calle 16/7ma. Ave. | tel. 07 2 04 15 43, 07 2 04 15 47 | daily 10am–3pm, shops to 6.45pm, restaurant noon–midnight*

WHERE TO STAY

INSIDER**TIP** CASA ALBERTO Y LIDYS CASTELLANOS

Travellers staying with Alberto are served Cuban history right from the horse's mouth. As Che Guevara's bodyguard he spent time in Bolivia, was imprisoned in Argentina and is now living with his wife Lidys, a gifted cook, in Havana in the house where Che once got married. *1 en-suite room with air-conditioning. | Calle 35 no. 1474 | betw. 26/28 | Nuevo Vedado | tel. 07 833 74 95 | casastellano@ gmail.com | Budget*

COMODORO

Alongside traditional hotel service (460 rooms, pool) this apartment hotel right by the ocean and entirely renovated in 2006 offers independent living in 18 apartments and 318 bungalows. Attractive anti-aging programmes include hydromassage and gymnastics sessions, as well as full-body treatments. *Av. 3ra/Calle 84 | Miramar (Playa) | tel. 07 2 04 55 51 | www.cubanacan.cu | Moderate–Expensive*

HABANA RIVIERA ⚲ (U A1) (𝄢 a1)

At this hotel you'll enjoy a fabulous sea view across the Malecón. The attractions on offer include the *Copa Room* salsa bar. *352 rooms | Vedado | Malecón/Paseo | tel. 07 8 33 40 51 | www.hotelhavana riviera.com | Moderate–Expensive*

NACIONAL DE CUBA ⭐ (U B2) (𝄢 b2)

Cast-iron elevator grilles and luxurious dining rooms and salons: built in 1930 with mafia monies, this top-notch establishment welcomed Hollywood stars such as Errol Flynn, Marlon Brando and Ava Gardner – before the revolution, of course. The *Cabaret Parisien* puts on a top revue show. *427 rooms | Vedado | Calle O/ corner 21 | tel. 07 8 73 35 64 | www.hotel nacionaldecuba.com | Expensive*

SOL-MELIÁ/TRYP HOTELS

The *Melía Cohiba* with its chic INSIDER**TIP** *Habana Café* – daily dance show, then the dance floor opens to all spectators *(8pm–2.30am, minimum consumption 10 CUC)* – is the number one place to be in Vedado *(462 rooms | Paseo | betw. Calle 1a/Calle 3a | tel. 07 33 36 36 | Expensive)*; the latest draw is the *sushi bar* in the *El Abanico* hotel restaurant *(Mon–Sat 7–1am | Expensive)*. You'll find the flagship of the Spanish hotel chain, the *Melía Habana*, in Miramar *(397 rooms | 3ra | betw. 76/80 | tel. 07 2 04 85 00 | Expensive)*. The former social hub of Havana, the *Habana Libre* Tryp hotel, with a top cabaret and the Turquino club on the top floor, also belongs to the Melía group *(569 rooms | Vedado | Calle L/Calle 23 | tel. 07 55 40 11, 07 33 38 04 | Expensive)*; for all: *www.solmeliacuba.de*

INFORMATION

MINTUR

HQ of the Cuban tourist information. *Calle 110 no. 318 e | betw. 3ra and 5ta | Miramar (Playa) | tel. 07 2 04 55 55, and 07 2 06 97 78 | www.infotur.cu*

HAVANA'S EAST AND SOUTH

Mostly within the city limits, these beaches provide the favourite weekend escape for Havana's residents.

Totalling some 60km/37mi, the beaches east of Havana are known as ★ ● *Playas del Este*. You can reach the first, narrow *Playa Bacuranao*, from the Malecón through the tunnel and on the Vía Blanca in 20 minutes. The widest, *Playa Santa María*, has developed into a small tourist centre. Half-way to Matanzas – before you get to the country's highest bridge, the 112m/367ft *Puente Bacunayagua* spanning the *Valle Yumurí* – you'll discover the *Playa Jibacoa* with an all-inclusive hotel.

Havana's 'green belt' spreads across the south. Here you'll find the international airport, the extensive recreation area of the *Parque Lenín* and the golf club. A big draw in the southeastern suburb of San Francisco de Paula is the Hemingway Museum.

SIGHTSEEING

MUSEO HEMINGWAY ★ ●

Hemingway's house on the edge of Havana is approx. 20 minutes' drive south of the Old Town. Furniture, hunting trophies, countless books, photos, documents and private mementoes – all has been left the way Ernest Hemingway (1899–1961) himself once left it. The writer purchased the Finca La Vigía in 1940. *Finca La Vigía San Francisco de Paula | daily 10am–5.30pm | admission 3 CUC*

MUSEO HISTÓRICO DE GUANABACOA ●

Comprehensive museum telling the story of Santería, Abakuá and the Palo Monte religion. Ceremonial objects, amongst them one of the last human skull drums. Traditionally, the Guanabacoa and Regla quarters of the city (opposite each other) are centres of Afro-Cuban cults. *José Marti 108 | betw. San Antonio/Versalles | Tue–Sat 10am–6pm, Sun 9am–1pm | admission 2, guided tour 1, photo permit 5, video 25 CUC*

Creative cosiness as it should be: the writer's living room at Museo Hemingway

FOOD & DRINK

LA TERRAZA

A large bar, festively decked tables with a view of the water, on the walls photographs of Hemingway: since the days when the great man ate and drank here, the small eatery has become a tourist attraction in Cojímar. With the restaurant the whole village benefits from its famous regular, who launched his boat for fishing trips from here. The fishing village has erected a monument to him at they quay. The restaurant specialises in seafood. *Cojímar | Calle Real 161 | betw. Montaña/ Candelaria | tel. 07 93 92 32, 07 93 34 86 | daily 11am–11pm | Moderate–Expensive*

WHERE TO STAY

APARTHOTEL ISLAZUL LAS TERRAZAS

Good-value apartments for a few relaxing days on the most beautiful beach of the Playas del Este. 82 apartments with TV, restaurant, pool. *Santa María del Mar | Ave. de Las Terrazas | betw. 10 und Rotonda | tel. 07 97 13 44 | www.islazul.cu | Budget–Moderate*

SUPERCLUB BREEZES JIBACOA

All-inclusive club for couples, singles and families with children over 13 years of age. *240 rooms | Playa de Jibacoa | tel. 047 29 51 22 | www.superclubscuba.com | Expensive*

A SHORT HOP BY PLANE FROM HAVANA

ISLA DE LA JUVENTUD

(121 D–E 5–6) (ⓜ C–D 3–4)

Shipwrecks, pirate legends and a treasure found here nurture the legend that the 2419 sq km island once called Isla de Pinos (Pine Island) is the 'Treasure Island' immortalised in literature by R L Stevenson. For Castro it was his prison island.

Today, the *Presidio Modelo*, a mass prison inspired by US penitentiaries where Fidel did time after the failed storming of the Moncada Barracks, is a museum *(on the Nueva Gerona–Playa Bibijagua road | Mon–Sat 8am–4pm, Sun 8am–noon | admission 2 CUC)*. Later, Castro renamed the island *Isla de la Juventud* ('Youth Island'), turning it into a centre of youth exchange. Today many camps remain unfilled; tourists are intended to fill the gap. *Nueva Gerona* (pop. 33,000) has a ferry port, a few peso eateries, amongst them the Chinese-inspired *El Dragón* restaurant *(Calle 39 | betw. 27/28 | tel. 046 32 44 79 | daily noon–10pm | Budget)*, a number of *casas particulares* and the hotels *Rancho del Tesoro (35 rooms | Ctra. La Fe, km 2.5 | tel. 046 32 30 35, Budget)* and *Villa Isla de la Juventud (Ctra. La Fe, km 1.5 | 20 rooms | pool | tel. 046 32 32 90 | Budget)*. Two museums are worth seeing: the *Museo Finca El Abra* on the edge of town *(Ctra. de Siguanea, km 2.5 | Tue–Sat 9am–4pm, Sun 9am–noon)*, where José Martí recuperated from his prison term in Havana in 1870, and the *Museo Municipal (Parque Central | Tue–Sat 9am–6pm, Sun 9am–1pm | both 1 CUC admission)*. If you want to go for a dip, you'll find the black sand of *Playa Bibijagua* to the east.

The most beautiful beach lies 60km/37mi outside the town in a nature reserve on the southern coast that can only be visited with a guide or written authorisation. There are caves with pre-Columbian rock paintings: the *Cueva de Punta del Este* and *Cueva Finlay*. Trips can be arranged through *Ecotur (Calle 39 | betw. 24/26 | tel. 046 32 71 01)*. Divers will find their needs met at the *El Colony hotel, Centros de Buceo (77 rooms | Ctra. Siguanea, km 42 | tel. 046 39 81 81 | www.hotelelcolony. com | Budget)*. The 56 diving spots are scattered around the Punta Francés.

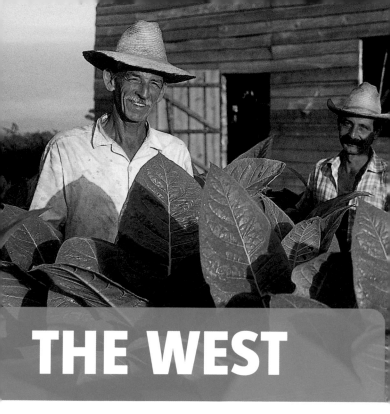

THE WEST

Apart from a few exceptions, such as Varadero, not the coasts and beaches, but mountain ranges and other areas are the best option for day trips or as a base for your holiday in the west. The nearest to the capital of Havana is the Sierra del Rosario, up to 800m/2600 ft high. It is home to many rare species of plants and animals that only occur on Cuba, and was declared a Unesco biosphere reserve in 1985.

Back in the 19th century, Americans were already taking (spa) holidays in San Diego de los Baños, where the Sierra del Rosario turns into the Sierra de los Órganos, long before the 1920s, when they chose Varadero as their new favourite spot. The mountain ranges mark the beginning of the tobacco province of Pinar del Río with the eponymous capital. Here, the best soils and most famous *vegas* (tobacco cultivation areas) of the world of cigars join the greatest scenic attraction in Cuba, the limestone mountains called *mogotes* in the Valle de Viñales, as well as another Unesco biosphere reserve, the Guanahacabibes National Park on the peninsula of the same name, Cuba's westernmost point. No less exciting destinations await east of Havana. The Vía Blanca takes you to Cuba's most famous resort: Varadero. And the Autopista Central shows the way to the Caribbean's largest swamp area, the Ciénaga de Zapata, where crocodiles and in the coastal waters manatees find respite from human intervention.

Photo: Tobacco planters in Pinar del Río

Look forward to forests, imposing limestone mountains, tobacco fields, jungle-like swamps and the famous beach of Varadero

PINAR DEL RÍO

(120 C4) *(ﾉ C3)* **Pinar del Río is a busy provincial capital, with a small-town atmosphere despite its 140,000 inhabitants.**

Pretty houses with arcades giving on to the Calle Martí are a testimony to the former wealth of small-scale tobacco farmers from the surroundings, the ex-

tensive growing area for the world's best tobacco. To this day, planters work for themselves here, resulting in a confident, down-to-earth kind of people.

SIGHTSEEING

FÁBRICA DE GUAYABITA

Using time-honoured recipes, a delicious liqueur is produced here from the guava fruit and sold. *Calle Isabel Rubio 189 | tel. 048 75 29 66 | Mon–Fri 9am–4.30pm, Sat/Sun 9am–1pm | guided tour 1 CUC*

On the beach of María la Gorda, Caribbean holiday dreams become reality

FÁBRICA DE TABACOS FRANCISCO DONATIÉN ●

Watch the *tabaqueros* at work and buy their products. *Calle Maceo 157 | Mon–Fri 9am–noon, 1–4pm, Sat 9am–noon | guided tour 5 CUC*

PALACIO GUASH/
MUSEO DE CIENCIAS NATURALES

The doctor Francisco Guash Ferrer immortalised himself by building in the curious mix of styles seen at Palacio Guash (1909). Amongst the attractions on show at the natural history museum housed here today are malformations preserved in spirit and a tyrannosaurus rex figure in true size. *Calle Martí 202 | Tue–Sat 9am–5pm, Sun 9am–1pm | admission 2 CUC*

FOOD & DRINK

EL MESÓN

The fact that this *paladar* is popular with Cubans too speaks for its quality. *Martí 205 | betw. Pinares/Pacheco | tel. 048 75 28 67 | Mon–Sat noon–10pm | Budget*

RESTAURANT CABARET RUMAYOR

The smoked fried chicken is the speciality here. Rustic ambience, and a show from 11pm *(Tue–Sun | 5 CUC)*. *Ctra. Viñales | km 1 | tel. 048 76 30 07 | open for food daily 10am–10pm | Budget–Moderate*

WHERE TO STAY

CASA DE ELENA RABELO

Light modern *casa particular* in a quiet location on the edge of town, a 15-minute walk to Calle Martí. *2 rooms | Antonio Rubio 284 | betw. Méndez Capote/Coronel Pozo | tel. 048 75 42 95 | Budget*

PINAR DEL RÍO

Old, squat hotel built for foreigners with simple rooms, pool and car hire. The Viazul bus stops here. *149 rooms | Martí/Final | tel. 048 75 50 70 | Budget*

INSIDER TIP ▸ VUELTABAJO

Centrally located hotel, nicely decorated with works by local artists. *39 rooms | Calle Martí 103 | corner Rafael Morales | tel. 048 75 93 81 | www.islazul.cu | Budget*

WHERE TO GO

MARÍA LA GORDA (120 B5) (∅ B3)

The 143km/88mi of road from Pinar del Río south to María La Gorda (3 hrs, take care: some of the road is in a bad state) are worth exploring for

Considered the cradle of tourism on the island, it was already luring US citizens to Cuba in the 19th century. You can try the curative powers of the water in the *Club Balneario* at the Hotel Mirador *(30 rooms | Calle Final 23 | tel. 048 77 83 38 | www.islazul.cu | Moderate)*. The hotel offers day trips into the *La Güira* national park and to the **INSIDER TIP** ▶ *Cueva de los Portales*, Che Guevara's headquarters during the Cuban missile crisis.

SOROA (121 D3) (*ﬔ D2*)

The attraction of Soroa, half-way between Pinar and Havana, is the magnificent *orchid garden (daily 8am–5pm | admission 3 CUC)*. Over 700 species grow in this tropical paradise. The flowering period is between November and April. Guided tours last 30–45 minutes. The nearby ⤴ *Mirador de Venus* offers glorious views. Before you get there, a path leads to the 22m/72ft *El Salto waterfall (daily 8am–5pm | admission 3 CUC)*. Hotel: *Villa Soroa | 49 rooms | Ctra. Soroa, km 8 | tel. 048 52 35 56 | Moderate*

more reasons than one. For one thing, it starts out by passing the world's best tobacco-growing area, the *Vuelta abajo*, in the triangle between Pinar, San Juan y Martínez and San Luis. In the Cuchillas de Barbacoa of San Juan y Martínez you'll discover famous *vegas* (tobacco plantations) such as *Las Vegas de Robaina*, a family concern since 1845. In the south, the Guanahacabibes peninsula, with its biosphere reserve, arches like a high-heel boot around the Bahía de Corrientes. Adventurous travellers will be drawn to the lonely tip of the boot with the *Cabo San Antonio;* the only hotel here is the *Villa Gaviota Cabo San Antonio (16 rooms in cottages on the Las Tumbes beach | extensión 204 | tel. 048 77 81 31 | Budget)*. Divers and beach lovers head for the heel of the boot, to María la Gorda with its diving hotel *Villa María La Gorda (55 rooms | tel. 048 77 81 31 | www.gaviota-grupo.com | Moderate)*. Day visitors coming by Transtur buses (12 CUC) from Pinar del Rio pay a 5 CUC admission fee.

SAN DIEGO DE LOS BAÑOS
(121 D3) (*ﬔ C2*)

The entire region is criss-crossed by mineral-rich springs, and the most famous of them bubbles away in this spa resort.

★ **Mogotes**
Unique landscape with ancient limestone features in the Valle de Viñales → p. 54

★ **Mansión Xanadú**
Stay here if money is no object → p. 59

★ **Cayo Largo**
Island lovers will find several of them here → p. 60

★ **Ciénaga de Zapata**
The Caribbean's largest swamp area is a paradise for plants and animals → p. 60

MARCO POLO HIGHLIGHTS

VALLE DE VIÑALES

LAS TERRAZAS ⏰ (121 D3) *(𝄞 C–D2)*

With its lake framed by picturesque mountain slopes, this eco-tourism resort in the biosphere reserve of the Sierra del Rosario near Soroa (4km/2.5mi) is an idyllic sight. Highlight is the *Hotel Moka (26 rooms | Autopista 4, km 51 | Candelaria–Pinar del Río | tel. 048 77 86 00 | Moderate)*, integrated into the landscape in an original way. Tickets for the park *(4 CUC)* and guided trips are available from the new information centre *Puerto Las Delicias (tel. 048 77 85 55)*.

VALLE DE VIÑALES

(120 C3) *(𝄞 B–C2)* **The scenery of this national park in the Valle de Viñales (approx. 84 sq mi, 53km/33 mi north of Pinar del Río) lures visitors from all over Cuba.**

The gigantic residual limestone hills rising out of the flat red soil here are millions of years old. Hollowed out by subterranean streams and eroded on the outside into soft shapes, the famous ★ *mogotes* are a paradise for nature lovers, sheltering many endemic plants and birds. Travellers congregate at the small cosmopolitan town of *Viñales* (since 1607) with its many *casas particulares*.

SIGHTSEEING

CUEVA DEL INDIO

Pleasure boats ply the river that runs through the cave, Río San Vicente. If you want to spot thousands of bats on their collective flight out of the cave every evening, make sure to be at the exit of the cave at the *Ranchón campestre* for 5.45pm. *Daily 9am–10pm | admission 5 CUC*

MURAL DE LA PREHISTORIA

With a bit of imagination, looking at the colourful mural (1961) painted on the bare limestone wall of the *Dos Hermanos* mogote by Leovigildo González feels like

Modern art on the limestone mountain: the Mural de la Prehistoria

being at the bottom of a primeval sea *(daily 8am–7pm | 2 CUC)*. The *Mural de la Prehistoria* restaurant serves pork chops with *arroz moro (tel. 048 93 62 60 | daily | Moderate)*. *Ctra. al Moncada, km 1*

FOOD & DRINK

CASA DE DON TOMÁS
Good restaurant in an old wooden house. The house cocktail 'Trapiche' is delicious. *Calle Salvador Cisneros | tel. 048 79 63 00 | daily 10–22 | Moderate*

EL PALENQUE DE CIMARRONES
You'll reach this restaurant, decorated in the colours of the Santería deities and inspired by a slave settlement *(palenque)*, from the snack bar at the entrance through a cave corridor, 140m/155yd long. The idea is to evoke the *cimarrónes* (escaped slaves) who in colonial times would take refuge in this kind of mogotes cave. The restaurant *(tel. 048 79 62 90 | Budget)* is only open for lunch, the snack bar at the cave entrance 24 hours a day *(Sat from 10pm cabaret with 'Ritmo y Sabor de Cuba' show and disco till 2am)*. *Ctra. a Puerto Esperanza, km 36*

WHERE TO STAY

HOSTAL DE GLORIA
Centrally located *casa particular*. Two well-kept rooms share a bathroom, veranda, good food. *Orlando Nodarse 15 | tel. 048 79 60 17 | yandeisy@alba.fr.vega. ins.cu | Budget*

LOS JAZMÍNES
The number one in Viñales, meeting place for tourists from all over the world. The ☆ pool terrace affords a fantastic view of the valley of the mogotes. *78 rooms | Ctra. de Viñales, km 25 | tel. 048 79 62 05 | Moderate*

WHERE TO GO

INSIDER TIP ▶ CAYO JUTÍAS
(120 C3) *(ɷ B2)*
The uninhabited small beach island near Santa Lucía is only a 45-minute drive from Viñales and can be accessed by a 12km/7mi causeway (admission 5 CUC incl. drinks voucher). You will find a crystal-clear ocean and a long lovely beach, partly covered by mangroves. Restaurant *(daily 9am–7pm)*, snorkel equipment hire, boat trips to the neighbouring Cayo Megano.

CAYO LEVISA (120–121 C–D3) *(ɷ C2)*
Small beach island to the northeast of Viñales, accessible only by sea from Palma Rubia *(trip out daily 10am, back 5pm | 20 CUC)*. If you'd like to stay overnight, there's the *Villa Cayo Levisa (35 rooms | tel. 048 75 65 01 | www.cubanacan.cu | Moderate)*.

VARADERO

(122 C2) *(ɷ F2)* **One of the first tourists who came to Varadero, the Chilean poet Pablo Neruda, raved about the magic of 'the sparklingly electric coast', and the 'incessant shimmering of the phosphor and the moon'.**

Today, visitors come for different attractions: sun & fun and a good hotel deal. Some 50 all-inclusive hotels line a beach which is not only a classic, but also at about 20km/12mi Cuba's longest and widest. The easterly part of the beach is reserved for tourists. Not much has remained of Varadero's beginnings as a saline village: the Elvira church completed in 1880 *(Calle 47/ 1ra Ave.)* and the prickly monster on the Punta del Rincón Francés, a 500-year-old giant cactus. Tip for individual travellers: since 2010, Va-

radero has been allowed to offer private accommodation *(casas particulares)* and private restaurants *(paladares)*.

SIGHTSEEING

MUSEO MUNICIPAL
The displays in the small municipal museum in the Casa Villa Abreu (1921) include the fruit of the hicaco tree, which gave its name to the peninsula. *Calle 57/Playa | daily 10am–7pm | admission 1 CUC*

PARQUE JOSONE
Pretty recreation park with an artificial lake, botanical rarities, restaurants and open-air bars. *1a Ave. | betw. Calle 56 and 59*

RESERVA ECÓLOGICA VARADERO
Varadero's green lung spreads across over 17 sq mi between hotel gardens in the east of the Hicaco peninsula. The park includes the *Cueva de Ambrosia* with cult carvings from pre-Columbian times and by escaped slaves. A INSIDER TIP *Centro Visitantes* has information on hiking trails, for example to the giant cacti. *Autopista Sur | admission 3 CUC*

FOOD & DRINK

LAS AMÉRICAS/BAR MIRADOR
This gourmet restaurant, decked out in fine mahogany, is one of the top choices. For a stylish beginning, or ending, to your dining experience consider a visit to the ⚘ *Mirador panorama bar* on the upper floor for a fantastic 360-degree view. *Ave. Las Américas/Mansión Xanadú | tel. 045 66 77 50 | daily noon–4pm, 7–9.30pm, bar Mirador 10am–11.45pm | Expensive*

LA BARBACOA
Grill restaurant in a former villa. Musicians play Cuban songs. Beef, fish (incl. crayfish), chicken. *1a Ave./Calle 64 | tel. 045 66 77 95 | daily noon–11pm | Moderate–Expensive*

On Cuba's beach peninsula of Varadero, sun & fun take centre stage

BODEGÓN CRIOLLO

Good Creole fare and Cuban specialities. Try *potaje de frijoles negros* or the hearty *arroz congris*. *Calle 40/Ave. La Playa | tel. 045 66 77 84 | daily noon–1pm | Budget– Moderate*

INSIDER TIP SALSA SUÁREZ

Paladar with small front garden, where you will be spoilt in style by the delicious, good-value dishes of the day, which could include *eperlán* (fried pargo fish balls) prepared by cooks David and Reinaldo. *Calle 31 Nr. 103 | betw. 1ra and 3ra Ave. | tel. 045 61 38 61 | daily from noon (till the last guest leaves) | Budget*

SHOPPING

SHOPPING CENTRES

The *Centro Comercial Hicacos (Ave. 1ra | betw. Calle 44 and 46)* was established on the lower floor of the *Coppelia* ice palace. That's also where you'll find the

INFOTUR office. For a bigger selection, head for the *Plaza Américas (Autopista Sur, km 11)* with a few branded boutiques.

SOUVENIR MARKETS

Straw hats, t-shirts, jewellery and much more is on offer from the five markets on the Avenida 1ra: *corner Calle 12, corner Calle 15, corner Calle 46, corner Calle 47 and corner Calle 54.*

TALLER DE CERÁMICAS ARTISTAS

Recommended sales gallery and workshop of Cuban ceramics artists. Right next door you'll find the *Galería de Arte*, filled with knick-knacks and art objects. *1a Ave./Calle 60 | daily 9am–7pm*

SPORTS & ACTIVITIES

DELFINARIO

Dolphins perform aerial acrobatics, and you can swim with dolphins too. *Autopista Sur y Final | tel. 045 66 41 15 | daily 9am–5pm, shows at 11am and 3.30pm | admission 15 CUC*

DISCOVER TOUR – JEEP & BOAT SAFARI

Reliable operator offering exciting day trips into the backcountry – by jeep, horse and boat. The schedule includes a visit to a cave, a sugar plantation and an INSIDER TIP adventurous boat trip through the unspoilt tropical river landscape of the Río Canimar near Matanzas, which you may skipper on your own without a boat license. *Reservation in the hotels or under tel. 045 66 75 50 | www.nauticamarlin.com*

(CATAMARAN) SAILING

There are boats for hire in the Marina Gaviota. This marina is also the departure point for the *Aqua Ray Tour* through the mangrove wilderness of

the island opposite *(daily 9am–4pm)*, catamaran trips into the island world east of Hicaco (Diana Cay, Romero Cay, Cayos Blancos, Piedra del Norte Cay) and fishing trips. *Marina Chaplin | Ctra. Las Morlas, km 12 | tel. 045 66 84 40 and 045 66 78 64*

DANCING

Clases de baile, instruction in Cuban dance, is on offer through the Cuban organisation *Paradiso Turismo cultural Artex (Calle 26 Nr. 106 | betw. 1ra and 2da | tel. 045 61 25 06, 045 61 47 59).* You train in blocks of three hours; after the first session, couples are given a free CD with Cuban music; if you come for more than two, you'll receive a diploma. *Reservation also through the hotels*

VARADERO GOLF CLUB

18-hole course at Mansión Xanadú. *Greenfee from 48 CUC (if booked at the hotel) | tel. 045 66 73 88 | www.varadero golfclub.com*

ENTERTAINMENT

BAR CAFÉ BENNY MORÉ

Friendly small rendezvous away from the hustle and bustle, ideal for a nightcap, sometimes to the tune of live Cuban music. *Camino del Mar | betw. Calles 12 and 13 | daily 11am–2am*

CABARETS

Discover a top dance revue at the *Varadero Internacional hotel (Ctra. Las Américas | tel. 045 66 70 38 | daily 9pm | incl. dinner 40, show/disco only 25 CUC).* One rival now is the 'paradise below the stars', the fantastic open-air arena of the *Tropicana Varadero* near Matanzas *(Autopista Matanzas–Varadero, km 4.5 | tel. 045 26 55 55 | Tue–Sun 8.30pm | from 39 CUC).*

MAMBO CLUB

Club for retro lovers: the preferred decade of these Cuban musicians is the 1950s. *Ctra. Las Morlas, km 14 | tel. 045 66 82 43 | daily 10pm–3am | admission 10 CUC*

PALACIO DE LA RUMBA

The largest club in the country puts on all kinds of rhythms. *Ctra. de las Américas, km 4 (where it finishes in a dead end) | daily 10pm–4am, Sun 4pm matinée for adolescents | tel. 045 66 75 52 | admission 10 CUC*

WHERE TO STAY

Around 50 large hotels (mainly with all-inclusive deals) are spread over the Hicacos peninsula, starting at Punta Arenas in the west to Punta Francés in the east. The fanciest establishments can be found on the eastern part of the peninsula, many of them Spanish (in a joint venture with Cuban hotel companies): four *Iberostar Resorts* (of which three are 5-star luxury hotels, *www.iberostar.com)*, eight hotels belonging to the *Sol-Meliá* group (including the 5-star brands *Paradisus* and *Tryp, www.meliacuba.com)* and three *Barceló resorts (www.barcelo.com).* Other players include *Blau Hotels (www. blauhotels.com), Sandals Resort (www. sandalshicacos.com), Hotetur (www. hotetur.com)* and *Globalia Varadero 1920 (www.globalia-hotels.com).*

BREEZES

Couples, singles and families with children over the age of 14 can choose between two superclub hotels: the *Breezes Varadero (270 rooms)* and the *Breezes Bella Costa (396 rooms).* Both: *Ctra. Las Américas, km 3.5 | tel. 045 66 70 30 | www.superclubscuba.com | Expensive*

BRISAS DEL CARIBE

All-inclusive complex on a quiet stretch of the beach bordered by a cliff. Very popular especially with the younger set. *440 rooms | Ctra. La Morlas, km 12 | tel. 045 66 80 30 | www.hotelesoasis.com |* Expensive

MANSIÓN XANADÚ ★

The marble baths with art nouveau and art deco taps, which the patron owner of the die villa, DuPont, just couldn't resist, can be enjoyed by hotel guests these days. Accommodation rates include breakfast and the green fee for the

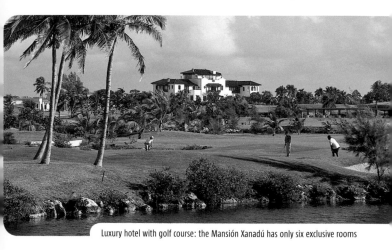

Luxury hotel with golf course: the Mansión Xanadú has only six exclusive rooms

CLUB KAWAMA

Individual living in dune villas from the 1950s and 1970s. *235 rooms | Ave. 1ra/ Calle O | tel. 045 61 44 16 | www.gran-caribe.com |* Moderate–Expensive

CLUB PUNTARENA

Run by the Cuban Gran Caribe company, this relaxed establishment is situated on the beach of the peninsula's western tip. *255 rooms | Ave. Kawama Final | tel. 045 66 71 25 | www.gran-caribe.com |* Expensive

HERRADURA

Good-value hotel on the beach, yet near the centre of town. *75 rooms | Ave. de la Playa | betw. 35/36 | tel. 045 61 37 03 | www.islazul.cu |* Budget

golf course in front of the entrance. The American industrialist DuPont de Nemours had this house built in the 1930s as a summer residence. *6 rooms | Ave. Las Américas, km 8.5 | tel. 045 66 84 82 | www.varaderogolfclub.com |* Expensive

BE LIVE LAS MORLAS/TURQUESA

Both all-inclusive complexes are situated right on the beach: the young *Las Morlas (143 rooms | Ave. Las Américas/A | Reparto La Torre | tel. 045 66 72 30 |* Moderate) near the town, and the *Turquesa (268 rooms | Ctra. Los Taínos | tel. 045 66 84 71 |* Expensive) 8km/5mi east (both *www.belivehotels.com).*

INSIDER TIP VILLA MARGARITA

Named after the friendly owner, this *casa particular* has a nice and quiet location

and offers three en-suite rooms with air-conditioning and safe, and there is a small flowering garden too. *Calle 22 and 3ra Ave. | tel. 045 61 42 12 | Budget*

WHERE TO GO

CÁRDENAS (122 C2) (*ØØ F2*)
Situated 18km/11mi southeast from Varadero, the town (pop. 70,000), once famed as 'city of the carriages', is worth visiting for its unvarnished Cuban flair. The biggest sights are the first monument to Columbus erected on the island (in Parque Colón) and the INSIDERTIP *Museo Oscar María de Rojas (Plaza San José Echeverría | Tue–Sat 10am–6pm, Sun 9am–noon | admission 5 CUC)*, with its collection of cultural and natural exhibits.

CAYO LARGO ⭐ (122 B–C5) (*ØØ E–F4*)
This is the southernmost of a number of islets between the Zapata peninsula and the Isla de la Juventud: Cayo Largo covers only 15 sq mi *(only accessible by*

air, as a day trip from Varadero). Many reckon this to be the most beautiful spot on Cuba, because the Caribbean Sea is so present here, the beach so white and as long as the entire island: 25km/15mi. If you'd prefer a sand bank for your sunbathing, take a boat across to *Playa Sirena*. Ferries also serve the palm-fringed beach of *Avalos*, the iguana island of *Cayo Iguana*, the snorkelling paradise of *Cayo Rico* and the sea-bird colony of *Cayo Pájaro*. The most luxurious hotel on the island is the *Sol Cayo Largo (296 rooms | tel. 045 24 82 60 | www.solmeliacuba. com | Expensive)*. The 53 palm-covered beach cabañas of the *Villa Lindamar hotel (tel. 045 24 81 11 | Moderate)* occupy a location on the edge of the hotel zone.

CIÉNAGA DE ZAPATA ⭐ (122 B–C3) (*ØØ E–F3*)
Cuba's most important wetlands in ecological terms stretch across the entire Ciénaga de Zapata peninsula and are criss-crossed by rivers and lagoons. Its dense mangrove vegetation provides a habitat for rare water birds and plants. The gateway to this huge area is *La Boca* on the *Laguna del Tesoro*. You can visit a

LOW BUDGET

▶ Ply all hotels and beaches of Varadero all day long for only 5 CUC? It's possible with the *hop-on-hop-off* buses. And the Matanzas–Varadero day ticket is only 10 CUC.

▶ Don't be afraid of internet bookings: if you want to take advantage of cheap all-inclusive hotels, you'll have to comb their websites or the major travel bookings portals (e.g. *www.expedia.com* or *www.expedia. co.uk*) for special deals – they're only available online!

La Boca on the Laguna del Tesoro is the gateway to the Ciénaga de Zapata wetlands

crocodile farm and try the meat of the animals kept for slaughter (daily 8am–4.30pm | admission 5 CUC). There are also supposed to be a large number of crocs in the wild still. The main destination for boat trips from La Boca is the Indian village of Guamá (see p. 99).

GIRÓN/BAHÍA DE COCHINAS (122 C3–4) (⬛ F3)

Deep in the south of the Matanzas province (which includes Varadero), the famous Bahía de Cochinas (Bay of Pigs) cuts deep into the land, flanked by the Ciénaga de Zapata, and towards the Caribbean coast the wild Playa Girón with the village of Girón. This is where mercenaries hired by exiled Cubans landed in 1961, in order to liberate Cuba from communism. The Museo de la Intervención (daily 8am–5pm | 2 CUC) and 48 stone monuments for the fallen commemorate the failed invasion. Hotel: Playa Girón (287 rooms | tel. 045 98 41 10 | Budget). The water in the rock basins of INSIDER TIP Caleta Buena, 8km/5mi east of Playa Girón (daily 10am–5pm | 12 CUC incl. drinks and food) runs crystal clear.

MATANZAS (122 B2) (⬛ E–F2)

The view of the pretty curved bay of Matanzas, 30km/18mi west of Varadero, quickly captivates visitors to the capital (pop. 643,000) of the Matanzas province. The small centre of the former sugar port boasts old palaces such as the Palacio del Junco, where the comprehensive Museo Histórico Provincial (provincial museum | Calle 83 | betw. 272 and 274 | Tue–Sat 9.30am–2pm, 1–5pm, Sun 9am–noon | admission 2 CUC) documents all periods. Diagonally across, the Teatro Sauto (1862, Plaza de Vigía) is a testimony to the sugar barons' appreciation of the arts at the time. Climbing into the city centre, Calle 83 leads directly to the old Triolet pharmacy, today the Museo Farmacéutico (Calle 83 no. 4951 | Mon–Sat 9am–6pm, Sun 10am–2pm | admission 3 CUC), a feast for the eyes of retro lovers. Attractions outside the city include the Cuevas de Bellamar (see Travelling with Children), the Río Canimar (boat trips from 30 CUC) and the nearby Tropicana open-air stage (advance ticket sales in the Varadero hotels).

THE CENTRE

The heart of Cuba sits like a buffer between cosmopolitan Havana to the west and Caribbean-feel Santiago to the east: quiet and rural in the south, slow-paced and down-to-earth around the Escambray range of low mountains. In nearby Santa Clara Che Guevara's successful offensive once helped the revolution to victory.

Reservoir lakes lend the mountainous landscape a touch of melancholy, which quickly dissipates on the southern coast. Cienfuegos, the former sugar port of the south, boasts a shiny new town centre and vibrant urban life. Rising on a hill only an hour's drive further south, Trinidad is a colonial gem where churches and residential palaces tell of the faded glory of the sugar boom of the early 19th century. And Camagüey, Cuba's 'golden heart' and third-largest city, captivates visitors with its lively mix of the past and contemporary culture.

Modern times rule up in the north, where the Archipiélago de Camagüey, connected by two land bridges with the main island, unfolds along the coast. Here, first-class holiday resorts have turned Cayo Coco, Cayo Guillermo and Cayo Santa María into attractive tourist destinations. At the eastern end of the chain of islands named 'Jardines del Rey' back in the 17th century in honour of the Spanish King, Playa Santa Lucía is a popular holiday destination, not only for divers and nature lovers.

Photo: Playa Ancón near Trinidad

Cayos and colonial atmosphere: experience nature and water sports, or take an inspiring stroll on the historic cobbles of an old quarter

CAMAGÜEY

(125 D3) *(K4)* **Since Unesco declared the historic core of the city (pop. 300,000) a World Heritage site in 2008, Camagüey has morphed into a confident beauty with colonial houses, shops, bars and restaurants.**

The city's symbol are *tinajones*, large terracotta jars once used by the wealthy to collect rainwater in the rainy season. Diego Velázquez founded the city in 1515,

WHERE TO START?
CITY Plaza de los Trabajadores: The name 'Labourers Square' is a bit misleading. This might be where Camagüey's heart beats, yet more in the sense of creativity and zest for life. Start off with great art in the Casa de Cultura (blue building), and browse the small stalls and shops in nearby Calle Maceo. The latter leads into República, where you'll find all the important agencies.

The equestrian statue in Camagüey honours freedom fighter Ignacio Agramonte

giving it the name Santa María Puerto Príncipe. At that time, the city was on the coast. However, due to pirate attacks and the marshy surroundings, it was moved in 1516 to the banks of the Río Caonao and in 1528 further inland, to its current position. In 1923, Camagüey received the name it bears today, taken from a cacique chieftain. A Spanish upper class achieved prosperity through sugar-cane cultivation and cattle-raising, and showed it in a vibrant cultural life. Camagüey is home to the poet Nicolás Guillén (1902–89), the scientist who discovered the carrier of yellow fever, Carlos F. Finlay (1833–1915) and the freedom fighter Ignacio Agramonte (1841–73). *www.caden agramonte.cu, www.pprincipe.cult.cu*

SIGHTSEEING

CASA DE CULTURA IGNACIO AGRAMONTE ●
The conspicuous blue post-art nouveau building (1928) with its pavilion-type roof on the Plaza de los Trabajadores hosts regular cultural events and always has works by contemporary artists on display. *Calle Popular 1*

PLAZA SAN JUAN DE DIOS
The pretty colonial square is framed by merchants' houses with restaurants and the **INSIDER TIP** gallery of artist Joel Jover as well as the *Antiguo Hospital de Dios*, once a hospital (1728), today the *Museum of Colonial Architecture,* with great views from its mirador *(Tue–Sat 9am–5pm, Sun 9am–1pm | admission 1 CUC).*

FOOD & DRINK

INSIDER TIP **EL BODEGÓN DON CAYETANO**
Popular gallery bar in a 19th-century house, confirming Camagüey's reputation as a city of artists. Good-value snacks, tasty pizzas. *Callejón de Soledad 256 | tel. 032 29 19 61 | daily noon–midnight | Budget*

EL OVEJITO
Specialising in lamb dishes, this excellent restaurant housed in a building dating from 1827 at the entrance to the Plaza

del Carmen has rustic furnishings and is always busy. *Calle Hermanos Agüero 152 | tel. 032 24 24 98 | Tue–Sun noon–9.45pm | Moderate*

ENTERTAINMENT

CASA DE LA TROVA
Live music featuring son and salsa bands. *Martí/Cristo 171 | tel. 032 29 13 57 | admission 3 CUC*

TEATRO PRINCIPAL
Built in 1850, this nicely restored theatre today again stages performances that are worth catching, for instance by the local ballet. *General Espinosa | tel. 032 29 30 48*

WHERE TO STAY

COLÓN
Unadulterated nostalgia rules, from the bar in the lobby to the furniture and the 47 comfortable rooms; the hotel first opened in 1926. *República 472 | betw. San José/San Martín | tel. 032 28 33 46 | www.islazul.cu | Budget–Moderate*

GRAN HOTEL
You won't find more central and better accommodation in Camagüey: built in 1939, the hotel has a good restaurant and a pool. *72 rooms | Calle Maceo 67 | tel. 032 29 20 93 | www.islazul.cu | Moderate*

WHERE TO GO

PLAYA SANTA LUCÍA (125 F3) (L–M4)
The small tourist resort named after its 21km/13mi beach is situated 110km/68mi northeast of Camagüey. Flamingos abound in the channel of Nuevitas Bay. At its estuary, *La Boca*, the *Playa Los Cocos* is a dream-like palm beach with restaurants. An additional draw for excursions is nearby *Cayo Sabinal* with a ruined fortress and the *Colón* lighthouse. Divers enthuse about the offshore reefs and (Nov–March) INSIDERTIP sharks that are used to being fed. *Scubacuba Shark Friends (www.cuba-diving.de)* is the diving base in the *Be Live Brisas Santa Lucía* holiday resort *(400 rooms | tel. 032 33 63 17 | www.belivehotels.com | Moderate–Expensive)*. Hotel tip: *La Escuela (30 rooms | Ave. Playa | tel. 032 33 63 10 | Budget)* right on the beach is good value as it is a hotel college at the same time.

CIENFUEGOS

(123 D4) (G3) The 'Pearl of the South' receives visitors with the cosmopolitan ease of a port , the confidence of an industrial centre and a pinch of French flair brought over by settlers from the French colony of Louisiana.

★ **Cayo Coco**
A wild island and dream hotels
→ p. 68

★ **Museo Memorial del Ernesto Che Guevara**
Pilgrimage site in Santa Clara for all fans of the never-forgotten revolutionary → p. 70

★ **Palacio de Valle**
Visit the palace and enjoy crayfish between Moorish mosaics in Cienfuegos → p. 66

★ **Trinidad**
Fine views from the tower of the city museum across the heritage old quarter → p. 72

MARCO POLO HIGHLIGHTS

CIENFUEGOS

The provincial capital (pop. 140,000) lies in a deep bay, which was protected early on by a fortress. Founded in 1819, and soon connected to the Cuban railway network, it rose from the mid-19th century to be the most important sugar port in the south. The city's former wealth is reflected in the villas on the Punta Gorda

Splendid: Palacio de Valle in Cienfuegos

peninsula and the Paseo El Prado boulevard. The historic centre entered the Unesco list of World Heritage sites in 2004.

CASTILLO DE JAGUA
The fortress (1745) used to protect the narrowest point of Cienfuegos Bay from Jamaican pirates. The jetty in front of the *Pasacaballo* hotel is the departure point for boats across.

PALACIO DE VALLE ★
Gothic, Napoleonic neo-classical and Moorish elements come together in this opulent villa, built between 1913 and 1917 for the Asturian-born sugar baron Acisclo del Valle Blanco. The Italian architect Alfredo Colli worked with Arabic, French, Italian and Cuban craftsmen. Superb views from the rooftop terrace. The rooms on the ground floor are used as a restaurant *(Ave. 0/Calle 37 | Punta Gorda | tel. 043 55 12 26 | restaurant daily noon–10pm, Mirador bar 10am–10pm | Moderate–Expensive). Visit of the house 1 CUC (incl. cocktail)*

PARQUE MARTÍ
Generously laid-out, with a band-stand and chairs, surrounded by magnificent restored houses, the park is home to the classicist *Teatro Tomás Terry* (1890), the *Palacio Ferrer* with viewing tower, the *Museo Provincial (in front of the governmental palace | Tue–Sat 10am–6pm | admission 2 CUC)*, documenting the history of the city, as well as the *cathedral* (1833–69).

FOOD & DRINK

BOUYÓN
The aroma of grilled prawns, beef fillets or chicken lures passers-by as well as regulars into Marco's paladar. Old photos of Cienfogos as decor set the mood. *Calle 25 no. 5605 | betw. 56/58 | Wed–Mon noon–10pm | Budget*

CLUB CIENFUEGOS

Terrace with splendid views of the bay, international cuisine: the restored yacht club is once again an exclusive address. *Calle 37 | betw. 8/12 | Punta Gorda | tel. 043 5128 91 | daily 9am–3am | Expensive*

COVADONGA

The place to go for fans of paella. María learned the art of preparing this archetypal Spanish rice dish in Valencia. She is shown on a photograph showing her with Fidel Castro, who partook of some food here after the victorious revolution. INSIDER TIP Fine views of the bay from the *Parillada* cocktail bar. *Calle 37 | betw. 0/1ra (opposite Hotel Jagua) | tel. 043 51 69 49 | daily 9am–midnight | Budget*

ENTERTAINMENT

EL BENNY BAR

Popular DJ bar in the historic centre with live music. *Ave. 54 (pedestrian zone) no. 2904 | betw. 29/31 | tel. 043 55 11 05 | daily 10am–1am | admission 3 CUC*

WHERE TO STAY

INSIDER TIP HOSTAL BAHÍA

In Diana and Omar's *casa particular* you'll be living with a view of the bay. The house is decorated with works by a Cuban artist, and Omar is proving to be an ambitious cook. *2 rooms (en-suite, safe) | Ave. 20, corner 35 no. 3502 | Altos | hostalbahia@yahoo.es | Budget*

JAGUA

Traditional house in an old residential quarter on the Punta Gorda peninsula with pool, bar, restaurant and shop. *149 rooms | Calle 37 no. 1 | Punta Gorda | tel. 043 55 10 03 | Moderate–Expensive*

PALACIO AZUL

The 'blue palace' next to the yacht club gives you a big bang for your buck: fantastic location, large rooms with satellite TV and safe, plus a restaurant and bar. *7 rooms | Calle 37 no. 1201 | betw. 12 and 14 | tel. 043 55 58 28 | www.cubanacan. cu | Moderate*

LA UNIÓN

This finely restored three-storey city hotel has elegant rooms, a courtyard pool and a roof-top bar. *49 rooms | Calle 31/54 | tel. 043 55 10 20 | www.cubanacan.cu | Moderate*

WHERE TO GO

GUAJIMICO (123 E4) *(G3)*

A statue of an Indian greets drivers 42km/26mi east of Cienfuegos at the entrance to the *Villa Guajimici* hotel complex.

LOW BUDGET

▶ Souvenir shoppers can hunt for a bargain Tue–Sun between 8am and 5pm at the crafts market on *Plaza San Juan de Dios* in Camagüey.

▶ ● Every morning from 10am, the large flight of steps leading up to the *Casa de Música* next to the *Iglesia Parroquial de la Santísima* Trinidad in Trinidad hosts free live music; show from 10pm. *Calle Juan Manuel Márquez*

▶ For only 5 CUC you can use the *hop-on-hop-off* buses on the route between Trinidad and the pretty Playa Ancón all day long between 9am and 7pm.

The facilities boast a pretty location on a deep-cut bay, 54 bungalows scattered on the steep banks and a pool with panoramic views, but could do with a lick of paint (*Ctra. Trinidad, km 42 | tel. 043 54 09 46 | Budget*). The hotel can arrange boat and diving excursions, amongst other activities, and also organises hikes.

JARDÍN BOTÁNICO (123 D–E4) *(G3)*

280 types of palms, 23 kinds of bamboo, all in all some 2000 local and foreign plants can be seen in the botanical gardens founded in 1901 in collaboration with Harvard University. *Ctra. a Trinidad Central Pepito Tey | daily 8am–4pm | admission 2.50 CUC*

PLAYA RANCHO LUNA (123 D4) *(G3)*

Long white sandy beach, partly consisting of a slightly rougher-grained sand, between the Cubanacán hotels *Club Amigo Rancho Luna (222 rooms | tel. 043 54 80 12 | Moderate)* and the quieter *Faro Luna (46 rooms | tel. 043 54 80 20 | Budget)*, both a good 14km/8mi south of the city on the Ctra. Rancho Luna (km 18). There are a few *casas particulares* near the Faro Luna lighthouse, as well as a *Delfinario (Fri–Tue 8.30am–4pm | admission 10, swimming with dolphins 50 CUC)*.

JARDINES DEL REY

(124–125 C–D1) *(J–K 2–3)* **Those who don't touch down at the international airport of Cayo Coco can reach this central group of islands of the Archipiélago Sabana-Camagüey via Morón across a 16km/10mi causeway (pedraplén).**

At the barrier of the connecting causeway, you'll have to pay 2 CUC (and the same again on the way back) and show your passport. The 140 sq mi main island of ★ *Cayo Coco* has most of the hotels. To the east, bridges and causeways connect it with *Cayos Romano* and *Paredón Grande*, as yet unexploited by tourism, as well as to the west, with the friendly-sized *Cayo Guillermo* (5 sq km). The islands are said to have been given the name of *Jardines del Rey* ('Garden of the King') by Diego de Velázquez. Despite enthusiastic construction activity, there is untouched nature behind the hotels. Mangrove swamps and shrub forests shelter 360 kinds of plants and 200 endemic animal species, including the white ibis or *coco*, as the Cubans call this bird (hence the name of the island, *Cayo Coco*).

Endless beaches on Cayo Coco

SIGHTSEEING

PARQUE NATURAL EL BAGÁ
(124 C1) *(J3)*

Nature trails, folklore shows and animal enclosures with crocodiles, iguanas and flamingos are the attractions at this leisure and nature park in the west of Cayo Coco. *Ctra. a Cayo Guillermo | tel. 033 30 10 63 | daily 9am–5pm | price depends on the chosen activity (e.g. 18 CUC for birdwatching)*

FOOD & DRINK

SITIO LA GÜIRA

This reconstructed charcoal-burner settlement stages rusticity to please the tourists; still: the *Rancho Los Márquez* offers solid Creole fare. *Cayo Coco Ctra. a Cayo Guillermo, km 10 | tel. 033 30 12 08 | daily 9am–11pm | admission 2 CUC | Budget*

SPORTS & BEACHES

All the hotels cater for divers and run trips, e. g. a catamaran outing to neighbouring islands or 'Jungle Trips' through the mangroves. Of the nine beaches on Cayo Coco and three on Cayo Guillermo, INSIDER TIP Playa Pilar on Cayo Guiller-

mo is the most beautiful. With its blue-green waters, white sand and dunes it's so stunning that the hotels send out a miniature train here. Catamaran sailors will take you to the *Cayo Media Luna* or for a snorkelling trip to the reef. One of the dishes served at the restaurant *(daily 9am–5pm | Budget–Moderate)* is crayfish for 15 CUC.

WHERE TO STAY

Most hotels on the islands are all-inclusive holiday resorts and cheaper to book as part of a package beforehand rather than as a spur-of-the-moment booking. The biggest player, with five hotels on both of the Cayos islands is the Sol Melia group *(www.solmeliacuba.com);* very popular is the 5-star adult-only *Meliá Cayo Coco* luxury resort *(250 rooms in water bungalows | tel. 033 30 11 80);* 2008 saw the opening of the 4-star *Blue Bay Cayo Coco (158 rooms | tel. 033 30 23 50 | www.bluebayresorts.com);* parts of the *NH Krystal Laguna* (352 rooms | tel. 033 30 14 70 | www.nhkrystallagunahotel .com) occupy a lagoon close to the beach); the first hotel on Cayo Coco, inaugurated in 1993 by Fidel Castro himself, is the *Blau Colonial (458 rooms | tel. 033 30 13 11 | www.blauhotels.com) which has had a complete makeover since.* For an extensive range of sports included in your package, choose the *Iberostar Daiquirí* on Cayo Guillermo *(312 rooms | tel. 033 30 16 50 | www.iberostar.com).* All *Expensive*

MOTEL JARDÍN LOS COCOS

Originally only for Cubans, now tourists too may take up residence here. *24 rooms | Ensenada Bautista | Cayo Coco | tel. 033 30 81 31 | www.islazul.cu | Budget*

CIEGO DE ÁVILA (124 C2) *(J3–4)*

The provincial capital (pop. 106,000) was named after the first landowner of the region. The first thing you see driving in on the Carretera Central, far from the

SANTA CLARA

(124 A1) *(H3)* **The confident provincial metropolis (pop. 238,000), founded in 1691 by citizens from nearby Remedios, forms the centre of a tobacco and sugar region.**

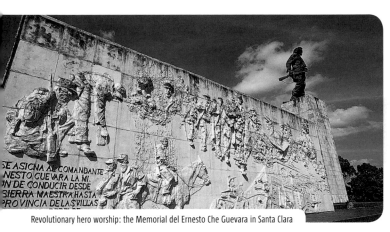

Revolutionary hero worship: the Memorial del Ernesto Che Guevara in Santa Clara

city centre, is the state-run *Ciego de Ávila hotel (117 rooms | restaurant, bar, pool, disco | Ctra. Ceballo | tel. 033 22 80 13 | Budget)*. Those who appreciate neoclassical architecture will enjoy a visit to the city centre. The pretty *Teatro Principal*, built in 1927, can be found near the cathedral on the main square.

MORÓN (124 C2) *(J3)*

Surrounded by sugar-cane fields and lagoons, the town 59km/36mi south of Cayo Coco is a rural oasis. A sculpture of a rooster is a reminder of the Andalusian origin of the first settlers. Pretty train station building (1923), good *casas particulares*, e.g. the *Casa Colonial Carmen (General Peraza 38 | betw. Felipe/ Céspedes | tel. 033 50 54 53 | gitccoco@ enet.cu | Budget)*.

Since visitors from all over the world have started to make the pilgrimage to the monument to Che Guevara on the edge of town, Santa Clara has developed into a tourist magnet. The city has also become the gateway to the new holiday resorts on off-shore *Cayería del Norte* further north, with the *Cayos Las Brujas, Ensenachos* and *Santa María*.

MUSEO MEMORIAL DEL ERNESTO CHE GUEVARA ★ ●

This monumental memorial was erected in 1988 to commemorate the 30th anniversary of Che Guevara's victory over the Batista troops on 31 December 1958 in this town. In 1997, the revolutionary's mortal remains, transferred from Bolivia, found their last resting place here. The exhibition includes Che's farewell letter and the pass-

port he used to enter Bolivia. *Ave. de los Defiles/Circunvalación | Tue–Sat 8am–9pm, Sun 8am–5pm | free admission*

MONUMENTO A LA TOMA Y ACCIÓN DEL TREN BLINDADO ●

Original wagons of the armoured train which was derailed by the rebels on 29 December 1958 on Che Guevara's orders, in order to force Batista's locked-in soldiers to surrender. *Calle Independencia/Calle Camajuani | Tue–Sat 5.30pm | admission 1 CUC*

FOOD & DRINK

CASA DEL GOBERNADOR

Pretty colonial house with a restaurant that will satisfy demanding palates. *Calle Independencia/corner Zayas | tel. 042 20 22 73 | daily 8am–10.45pm | Moderate–Expensive*

WHERE TO STAY

LOS CANEYES

For those who like to stay in natural surroundings outside the city: this resort, designed in Indian style, offers a pool, bar and disco. *95 rooms with TV, bungalows | Ave. de los Eucaliptos | tel. 042 21 81 40 | Moderate*

INSIDER TIP HOSTAL D'CORDERO

This casa particular of Orlando C Rodríguez is situated right in the heart of the action and fulfils many travellers' desires from TV to food in an ambience crammed with antique furnishings. *2 rooms | Calle Rol. Pardo 16 | betw. Maceo/Parque | tel. 042 20 64 56 | o_cordero2003@yahoo.com | Budget*

WHERE TO GO

CAYERÍA DEL NORTE (124 B1) *(J2–3)*

The western Archipiélago Sabana-Camagüey is accessed via Santa Clara, Reme-

dios and Caibairién across a 48km/30mi causeway (one way 2 CUC, don't forget to bring your passport!). Along the causeway, you'll pass the islands of *Cayo Las Brujas* and *Cayo Ensenachos*, before you reach the main island of *Cayo Santa María*. There are few hotels here so far, amongst them the exclusive *Royal Hideaway Ensenachos (506 rooms | www.occidentalhotels.com | Expensive)* with the affiliated ● *Cayo Ensenacho Royal SPA* on the beach of Cayo Ensenachos. Individual travellers may bed down at the *Villa Las Brujas hotel (cottages with TV, minibar, air-conditioning | 23 rooms | Cayo Las Brujas | tel. 042 35 00 23 | Moderate)* or stock up with provisions at the kiosk of the airport on Cayo Las Brujas, for a day maybe on the romantic INSIDER TIP Playa Perla Blanca at the biological station of *Punta Cerquita* on the largest island: Cayo Santa María is 13km/8mi long and 2km/just over 1 mi wide. This is where a number of top hotels have established themselves: the 4-star *Sol Cayo Santa María (300 rooms)* and the five-star *Meliá Las Dunas (925 rooms), Meliá Cayo Santa María & SPA (356 rooms)*. At Punta Madruguilla in the west you have the elegant *Meliá Buenavista Royal Service (104 junior suites, from 18 years of age)* – all are all-inclusive resorts owned by the Spanish Sol Meliá group *(www.solmeliacuba.com)*. A more recent arrival is the exclusive *Barceló Cayo Santa María Beach & Colonial Resort (www.barcelo.com), all Expensive.*

REMEDIOS (124 A1) *(H3)*

Its foundation date of 1514 makes Remedios one of Cuba's oldest towns. Remedios can also boast one of the most beautiful churches in Latin America: the altar of the INSIDER TIP Iglesia San Juan Bautista is entirely gilded *(admission 2 CUC)*. Also worth seeing is the *Museo de las Parrandas (Máximo Gómez 71 | daily 9am–noon,*

1–6pm | admission 1 CUC) with costumes from the town's fireworks and costume festival *(16/24 Dec)*. Reside in style at the *Hotel Mascotte* on the main square *(10 rooms | Calle Máximo Gómez 114 | tel. 042 39 51 44 | Moderate)* or in the private palace of *La Casona Cueto (2 rooms | Alejandro del Rio 72 | betw. E. Malaret/Máximo Gómez | tel. 042 39 53 50 | Budget)*.

TRINIDAD

(123 E4) *(H4)* ⭐ **Founded in 1513 by Velázquez, the town (pop. 36,000) forms a true heritage ensemble.**

The town's distinguishing features are its cobblestones (imported from Boston!), tall wooden doors and trellised windows, and its baroque church towers, in particular that of the former *Convento San Francisco* (1730). Trinidad acquired its wealth in the early 19th century, during the sugar boom. The liberation of the slaves and the War of Independence stopped the town's development short and Trinidad's port lost its important role. Declared a national monument in 1950 and a Unesco World Heritage site in 1989, Trinidad is one of Cuba's most important tourist attractions today, together with the *Valle de los Ingenios*, the valley of the sugar factories, in the town's hinterland.

SIGHTSEEING

MUSEO DE LA CIUDAD

Municipal museum in the former residence of sugar baron Cantero, with the kitchen giving onto the patio. The tower affords fine views across the rooftops of the town. *Simón Bolívar 423 | Sat–Thu 9am–5pm*

MUSEO ROMÁNTICO ●

The former palace of the Conde Brunet illustrates the luxurious way of life of the sugar aristocracy. *Calle F. H. Echerri 52/ Simón Bolívar | Tue–Sat 9am–5pm, Sun 9am–1pm | 2 CUC*

VALLE DE LOS INGENIOS

An emblematic presence in the sugarcane valley, also known as Valle de San Luis, is the 43.5m/141ft-high 19th-century bell tower in *Manaca Iznaga* near the road to Sancti Spíritus. One of its functions was to serve the supervision

Visiting Trinidad is like taking a trip into Cuba's colonial past

of slaves on the fields. Why not take a gentle trundle on the ● *tren de vapor* (steam train) through the sugar-cane fields *(daily from 9.30am from Estación de Toro in Trinidad | return trip 10 CUC)?*

FOOD & DRINK

LA CANCHÁNCHARA
Cosy meeting place for lovers of the eponymous drink made from honey, rum and lemon juice. *Rubén Martínez Villena 78 | daily 10am–8pm | Budget*

PALADAR ESTELLA
Hearty Cuban home-made fare. *Simón Bolívar 557 | tel. 041 99 43 29 | Budget– Moderate*

SHOPPING

LA CASA DEL ALFREDO
Long-established ceramics workshop. The masks painted in Santería colours make pretty souvenirs. *Andrés Berro no. 9 | betw. Avel Santamaría/Julio A. Mella*

WHERE TO STAY

LAS CUEVAS
Magnificent views across town and bay, museum cave and the **INSIDER TIP** cave disco Ayala *(Tue–Sun from 10pm).* The hotel lies on a slope behind the town. *109 rooms | Finca Santa Ana | tel. 041 99 67 08 | reservas@cuevas.co.cu | Moderate*

CASAS PARTICULARES
Recommended private accommodation: the hostals *Doctora Margarita (Calle Simón Bolívar 113 | betw. P. Zerquera/A. Cárdenas | tel. 041 99 32 26),* and *Sarah Sanjuán (Calle Simón Bolívar 266 | betw. F. Pais/José Martí | tel. 041 99 39 97)* both *Budget*

IBEROSTAR GRAN HOTEL TRINIDAD
Small 5-star oasis in the historic centre, with covered patio; show cooking, games room, internet café. *40 rooms | Calle Jose Martí 262 | betw. Lino Pérez/ Colón | tel. 041 99 60 73 | www.iberostar. com | Expensive*

WHERE TO GO

GRAN PARQUE NATURAL TOPES DE COLLANTES (123 F4) *(H4)*
From Trinidad, 18km/11mi of hairpin bends lead to Topes de Collantes (800m/2600ft) into a world of waterfalls, rivers, valleys and gentle heights supporting cedar, pine, teak, agnolia and mahogany trees, ferns, blossoms, hummingbirds and butterflies. Pick up tickets *(6.50 CUC),* trail maps and hiking guides from the information centre *(daily 8am– 5pm)* in front of the *Escambray spa hotel (www.gaviota-grupo.com)*.

PLAYA ANCÓN (123 F4) *(H4)*
The shuttle bus *(5 CUC per day)* will take you to *Playa Ancón* 11km/7mi south. The 4km/2.5mi pretty beach with its fine white sand is never crowded, despite the existence of a handful of holiday resorts, e.g. the all-inclusive *Brisas del Mar* hotel *(241 rooms | Ancón peninsula| tel. 041 99 65 00 | Expensive),* built in the style of a Caribbean village.

SANCTI SPÍRITUS (123 F4) *(H3)*
Founded in 1514, this colonial town (pop. 72,000) is an hour's drive from Trinidad (67km/41 mi). The *Iglesia Parroquial Mayor del Espíritu* in the centre is one of Cuba's oldest churches (1522). Refuel opposite, at the *Mesón de la Plaza* (solid Creole fare, *Máximo Gómez 34 | tel. 041 32 85 46 | daily from 10am | Budget).* Accommodation tip: *Hostal D'Martha (2 rooms | Calle Plácido 69 | betw. Tirso Marín/Calderón | tel. 041 32 35 56 | Budget).*

THE EAST

The people of eastern Cuba, *Oriente*, are said not to care much about who is governing in Havana and how. Oriente is Fidel Castro's home turf. His cradle stood near the Bahía de Nipe, a region that turns its back on the rest of Cuba, looking out to sea.

Here, a certain lack of submissive spirit has historical roots. In pre-Columbian times already large autonomous cacique (chieftain) empires existed here. Indian cemeteries, over 1500 years old, and other archaeological sites are evidence of this Taíno civilisation. The colonial age too started in the east: this was where Columbus first stepped ashore, where he planted the oldest still preserved wooden crosses in the soil, on the spot which was later to give rise to the first colonial town

in Cuba, Baracoa. The town became the seat of the governor – until he took a shine to Santiago de Cuba. The first slave ships moored off this coast, where the refugees from Sainte-Domingue, later Haiti, landed, kick-starting Cuba's coffee and sugar economy. Finally, nearly half a millennium after the Spanish had suffocated Indian resistance with the execution of the cacique Hatuey, it became the place where the plans for two revolutions were hatched.

Nature lovers can look forward to beautiful stretches of coastline: west of Santiago de Cuba, at Cuba's highest peak, Pico Turquino, the Sierra Maestra drops down to the steep coast of the Cayman Trough. In the farthest east, mountain ranges have created a coastline characterised by wild

Photo: Guantánamo Bay near Baracoa

From the birthplace of the country to islands, beaches and bays – from the cradle of the son sound to the 'landing place' of the revolution

coves and river estuaries which in the north changes into a landscape of karst mountains, bays and cayos. The main draw of the east, however, remains Santiago de Cuba, the 'home of Cuban music'.

BARACOA

(127 F4) (*ᗰ P6*) **The winding access drive via the La Farola mountain road gives an idea of the remoteness of Baracoa (234km/145mi from Santiago de Cuba).**

Still, this pretty and today rather compact town (pop. 82,000) at the foot of the distinctive *El Yunque* (560m/1837 ft) table mountain marks the beginning of Cuba's colonial history. It was here that in 1492, Columbus rammed a wooden cross into the ground. In 1511, Diego Velázquez, arriving from Santo Domingo (Dominican Republic) founded the island's first capital here. Today, the town is a centre of fishing, coffee and cocoa growing – and an oasis for independent travellers and nature lovers.

SIGHTSEEING

MUSEO ARQUEOLÓGICO PARAÍSO

On display in the three-part cave are finds from the Taíno period, as well as a skull considered to be the INSIDER TIP head of the Guamá cacique. *Reparto Paraíso | daily 8am–5pm | admission 3 CUC*

Cocoa is grown all around Baracoa

MUSEO MUNICIPAL

Housed in the *Fortaleza Matachín* (1739–42), this museum tells the history of the town and region. *Daily 8am–6pm | admission 1 CUC*

FOOD & DRINK

FINCA DUABA/EL CACAHUAL

Popular day-trip for nature lovers. Attractions on the *Finca Duaba* include the *El Cacahual (Budget)* restaurant, botanical gardens and a 270m/300yd *Sendero del Cacao* (educational cocoa trail). There is

also a good place for a dip in the sea nearby. *Ctra. Baracoa–Moa, km 2 | daily 8am–4pm*

FUERTE DE LA PUNTA

View of the strait across to Haiti, surrounded by old fortification walls; good grilled fish. *tel. 021 64 18 80 | daily noon–3pm, 6–11pm | Budget*

WHERE TO STAY

EL CASTILLO

The largest holiday hotel in town stands on the remains of an old fortress. *34 rooms | Calixto García Loma del Paraíso | tel. 021 64 51 65 | www.gaviota-grupo. com | Moderate*

HOSPEDAJE LA TERRAZA

Pleasant guesthouse with pretty roof terrace; meals can be arranged. *2 rooms | Maceo 235 | between Abel Díaz/Limbano Sánchez | tel. 021 64 38 57 | Budget*

VILLA MAGUANA

This small hotel, which will please individualists, occupies a beautiful position on two wild beaches. *4 rooms | Ctra. Baracoa–Moa, km 22 | tel. 021 64 51 65 | www.gaviota-grupo.com | Budget*

WHERE TO GO

GUANTÁNAMO (127 E4) (𝄐 O6)

Cuba's easternmost provincial capital (pop. 244,000) is no great beauty; still, colonial houses surviving in its core serve as a reminder of its foundation by French refugees from present-day Haiti. The place grew too fast following the establishment, in 1903, of a US base in the Bahía Guantánamo, a good 12km/7mi south. Originally limited, the lease has been extended since 1934, indefinitely. Fidel Castro is said never to have cashed

the annual cheques. Recently, the base became infamous as a zone exempt from normal civil law for questioning and incarcerating supposed and real Taliban fighters. Since then, the *Mirador de los Malones* restaurant has had a good (binocular-assisted) view of the base.

● The peasant women of Guantánamo were immortalised in José Martí's *Versos Sencillos*, (Simple Verses). In the early 1930s this cycle of poems was used by José Fernández Díaz as the lyrical base of his song Guantanamera, which went on to global fame and today forms part of every Cuban folklore band's repertoire.

PARQUE NACIONAL ALEJANDRO DE HUMBOLDT (127 E4) *(⚹ O–P5)*

Considered the last contiguous rainforest in the Caribbean, the huge area in Baracoa's hinterland shelters around 2000 plant and **INSIDER TIP** 90 bird species (the tocororo is one of them) and has been on the Unesco World Heritage list since 2001. Hikes (2–5 hrs) are only possible in a part of the park, and only with a guide, who will lead you to clear streams and stunning hidden beaches. Bookings in Baracoa through Cubatur *(Calle Maceo/corner Pelayo Cuervo | tel. 021 64 53 06 | various 5-hr trips 24 CUC)*.

HOLGUÍN

(126 B–C3) *(⚹ N5)* **The provincial capital (pop. 326,700) was named in the mid-16th century after the first Spanish landowner. With many parks and a few noteworthy buildings in the centre, including San Isidoro Cathedral (1720), the city lies between karst mountains enclosing the Mayabe Valley.**

The city's emblem is the *Loma de la Cruz* mountain. Its summit cross is reached by a set of 461 steps. On 3 May, the

INSIDER TIP Romerías de Mayo, this becomes a pilgrimage site for many faithful. However, the city shows no sign of excessive piety. People are full of life and open-minded, in particular since Holguín became the gateway to the *Parque Natural Colón* holiday region (Columbus Nature Park), bringing its fair share of tourists into town. Also known as *Costa Esmeralda*, this vacation region stretches across the bays of the northern coast, accessible via the good *Carretera a Guardalavaca*. This road ends at the *Playa Guardalavaca* where tourist development first began.

SIGHTSEEING

MUSEO DE CIENCIAS CARLOS DE LA TORRE

Cuba's biggest collection of snails and snail shells. *Calle Maceo 129 | between Martí/Luz Caballero | Tue–Sat 9am–10pm, Sun 9am–9pm | admission 1 CUC*

⭐ **Finca Mañacas**
The parental estate of Fidel Castro gives deep insights into his youth → p. 78

⭐ **Casa de Velázquez**
Santiago boasts Cuba's oldest house, today a colonial museum → p. 81

⭐ **Museo Casa de la Trova**
All the big stars have performed at this music bar in Santiago, now a museum → p. 83

⭐ **La Comandancia de La Plata**
The revolutionaries' hideout in the Sierra Maestra is great hiking terrain → p. 86

MARCO POLO HIGHLIGHTS

HOLGUÍN

WHERE TO STAY

CASA GONZÁLEZ HERRERA

Great for those who prefer to live in private accommodation and be independent: the holiday apartment on the upper floor allows for self-catering, has a car park and is situated only three blocks from the central Máximo Gómez road. *2 rooms | Victoria 68 | between Agramonte/ Garayalde | tel. 024 42 43 51 | Budget*

MIRADOR DE MAYABE A

Rustic-style hotel on the karst hill of Mayabe, with the best view across the city; pool, restaurant. Part of the set-up is the INSIDER TIP Mayabe museum finca. *24 rooms in villas | Alturas de Mayabe, km 8 | tel. 024 42 21 60 | Budget*

WHERE TO GO

BANES (127 D3) (∅ N5)

The area around Banes is known for its numerous pre-Columbian archaeological sites. In 1980, for example, the largest Indian cemetery in the Caribbean was found on the Chorro de Maíta, sheltering some 1000 skeletons up to 1500 years old. 62 of them can be seen at the *Museo Chorro de Maíta* opposite the reconstructed Indian village of *Aldea Taína (Ctra. Guardalavaca–Banes | Mon 9am–1pm, Tue–Sun 9am–5pm | village and museum 5 CUC)*. Numerous finds can be viewed in Banes (34km/21mi from Guardalavaca): in the *Museo Indocubano Baní (General Marrero 305 | Tue–Sat 9am–5pm, Sun 8am–noon | admission 1 CUC)*, which was named after the powerful cacique of the region, Baní. A rarity amongst the exhibits is a golden statuette showing Central American influence.

At the beginning of the last century Banes was practically owned by the US enterprise United Fruit Company. At this time Fulgencio Batista (1901–73), who would go on govern Cuba as a dictator, was born in the city. Batista's future arch-enemy Fidel Castro was born 25 years later, not too far away, in Birán. It was in Banes too that on 12 October 1948, Castro married Mirta Díaz-Balart, the mayor's daughter. In 1950, Mirta's brother Rafael, who later became Minister of the Interior under Batista, facilitated a meeting between Castro and the dictator. In 1953 – one year before Castro attempted to storm the Moncada barracks – his marriage was annulled. And in 1959, after the victory of the revolution, Mirta's brother founded the first anti-Castro organisation.

BARIAY PARQUE MONUMENTO NACIONAL (127 D3) (∅ N5)

16 Indian goddess statues, surrounded by Greek columns arranged in the shape of a ship's hull, are a reminder of 29 October 1492, when Christopher Columbus stepped ashore here. The monument in the big park was created in 1992 by Caridad Ramos Mosquera. The park (sign-posted) lies near Fray Benito. *Daily 10am–6pm | admission 8 CUC*

BIRÁN (126 C4) (∅ N5)

If you'd like to know where and how Fidel Castro passed the first 14 years of his life, visit his parents' ★ *Finca Mañacas* in this mountain village 66km/41mi east of Holguín. The estate comprises 26 buildings, amongst them the reconstructed first residence (burnt down in 1954), where Castro was born on 3 August 1926. The room that Fidel shared with brother Raúl is on view, as well as the cockfighting arena. *Finca Mañacas | daily 9am–5pm | admission 10, photo/video permit 10 CUC*

CAYO NARANJO (126 C3) (∅ N5)

The island in the large 'Orange Bay' (access by ferry) is a leisure paradise with

many facets: shows with dolphins and sea lions at the biggest crowd puller, *Acuario (see Travel with Children')*, pleasure trips by catamaran *(daily 9.15am)* and beaches for picnics and a dip. If you enjoy this kind of vibe, why not stay the night: at the *Villa Cayo Naranjo Hotel (2 suites | tel. 024 3 01 32 | www.gaviota-grupo.com | Budget);* the *Biráncito* bungalow is rather similar to Fidel Castro's parents' finca in Birán. *Ferry: Ctra. Guardalavaca, km 48*

INSIDER TIP CAYO SAETÍA
(127 D3–4) *(ฒ O5)*

The island, connected with the mainland by a causeway, is home to animals including gazelles, buffaloes, ostriches and antelopes living as they would in the wild *(admission 10 CUC | bring your passport!)*. Accommodation at *Hotel Villa Cayo Saetía (16 rooms | tel. 024 9 69 00 | Moderate–Expensive)*.

GUARDALAVACA (126 C3) *(ฒ N4–5)*
The name Guardalavaca ('look after the cow') might make you think this place might be a tad boring. But it's not that bad. The bungalows and hotels of the holiday village now look slightly tired, even if modernised several times already, and today are outshone by all-inclusive hotels on the neighbouring beaches. Yet the beach is still the most beautiful in the region. In order to stay in the game, a few smaller hotels were roped into the all-inclusive operation of the *Cubanacán (www.cubanacan.cu) hotel company;* for instance the *Club Amigo Atlántico (747 rooms in bungalows | tel. 024 301 80 | Moderate)*. The excellent *Brisas Guardalavaca (225 rooms | tel. 024 302 18 | Moderate)* is another. The dream beach, as well as the restaurants, the shopping drag, the car rental and the open-air disco *La Roca (Thu–Sat 10am–2am | admission incl. drinks voucher 3 CUC)* are open to anyone. An idyllic place to enjoy fine fish dishes with a view of beach and sea is **INSIDER TIP** *El Cayuelo (Playa Guardalavaca | tel. 024 307 36 | daily 9am–11pm | Budget–Moderate)*.

Straight out of a brochure: Guardalavaca Beach

PLAYA ESMERALDA (126 C3) (*⊞ N4–5*)
Just 4km/2.5mi west of Guardalavaca in a gently curved bay with fine white sand, this beach perfectly illustrates this coast's good reputation as a beach paradise. The Spanish Sol Meliá hotel chain *(www.solmeliacuba.com)* operates two ● all-inclusive mega hotels here: the *Sol Río de Luna y Mares (464 rooms | tel. 024 43 00 60 | www.solmeliacuba.com | Expensive)* and to the east the *Paradisus Sol Río Resort & Spa (354 rooms | tel. 024 43 00 90 | Expensive)*. You can visit the offshore reefs with the *Diving Center Sea Lovers (www.cuba-diving.de)*. A great attraction at the western end of the bay is the INSIDER TIP Los Guanos nature reserve with its well-signposted educational trail *(daily 8am–6pm | admission 6 CUC)*. Hearty Cuban fare is served at the *Conuco de Mongo Viña restaurant (tel. 024 307 48 | daily 9am–6pm | Budget)*

PLAYA PESQUERO (126 C3) (*⊞ N4–5*)
The white *Playa Pesquero* drops towards the turquoise waters of a bay west of the Bahía Naranjo. There are two Gaviota hotels *(www.gaviota-grupo.com)*: the *Playa Pesquero Resort (944 rooms | large spa area | tel. 024 305 30)* and the sporty *Playa Costa Verde (480 rooms | gym, kayaks, bikes | tel. 024 350 10)*. To the north, you also have the familiar *Blau Costa Verde* with its pretty landscaped lagoon *(250 rooms | tel. 021 350 10 | www.blauhotels.com)*, all *Expensive*.
Things get even quieter further east on the *Playa Turquesa* at the *Grand Playa Turquesa Resort (520 rooms | tel. 024 305 40 | www.occidental-hoteles.com | Expensive)*. Right nearby, on the way to the Playa Yuragunal, you'll find the information centre of the INSIDER TIP Bioparque Rocazul *(tel. 024 308 33 | daily 8.30am–5pm)*. Named after a blue rock that is found here, the park, extending over 2 sq mi to the *Bahía Naranjo*, offers hiking and horse-riding trails *(8 and 16 CUC/hr, respectively)*, mountain-bike routes *(15 CUC/hr)* and refreshment stops such as the *Finca Monte Bello (daily 8.30am–5pm | Budget)*.

SANTIAGO DE CUBA

(126 C5) (*⊞ N6*) **The narrow alleyways, parks and churches of Cuba's most vibrant and hottest city (pop. 490,000) spread across the hilly peninsula on a large deep bay.**

The city's narrow estuary towards the Caribbean is well protected: in front, acting like a stopper, lies the small *Cayo Granma* island, and on the cliff the *El Morro* fort guards the entrance as it did during the period of great danger posed by Jamaican pirates. The central meeting point in the city is the *Parque Céspedes*. Buildings with great historic associations face each other here: the city hall, where Fidel Castro once proclaimed the victory of the revolution from the balcony; the splendid *Hotel Casa Granda*, whose terrace is populated by tourists once again; the *Casa de Velázquez*, residence of the city founder and first island governor Diego Velázquez; and the imposing *cathedral* (founded in 1522, remodelled in 1922), where Pope John Paul II held a reconciliation service in 1998.
From 1524 Santiago de Cuba was the capital of the island, yet had to cede the title to Havana as early as 1607. What saved Santiago from falling into insignificance was the revolution on Haiti. At the time, many coffee and sugar farmers fled to Santiago de Cuba with their slaves. Their quarter, stretching south of the historical centre across the *Loma del*

Intendente, soon became known for the dances and songs of the slaves: performances that earned it the name 'Tivoli'. In his novel The Kingdom of this World, Alejo Carpentier tells us about this period in Santiago's life. In economic terms, Santiago de Cuba and the whole of Cuba benefited from French know-how in cultivating sugar-cane and coffee. The most famous heritage however is music. In the way that the same French immigrants turned New Orleans into the capital of jazz, they made Santiago de Cuba the metropolis of son and bolero. In some houses of the Barrio Tivoli, you can still watch the original *tumba francesa* from the time of the French Revolution being danced. On the other hand, Fidel Castro learned at the city's old colonial Jesuit college – with 'very strict teachers', as he put it – values such as discipline which were to make him the victor in the Cuban revolution. Together with its exuberant

> **WHERE TO START?**
> **Parque Cespedes:** the best starting point for a wander around town, for making all the important arrangements (bank and Infotur office are to the right and left of the cathedral) and to get a first impression of the place. A few paces lead you to the Museo Casa de la Trova, and the always-vibrant Plaza de Dolores is quickly reached on foot too.

carnival in July, contrasts like this make Santiago what it is.

SIGHTSEEING

CASA DE VELÁZQUEZ ★

One look at the wooden grilles of the balcony give the house away as a colonial gem: the Casa Diego Velázquez was

The heart of Santiago de Cuba: the cathedral near Parque Cespedes

built between 1516 and 1522 for Cuba's first governor. The ground floor, which served as the commander's office, held the smelting oven for looted gold. The upper storey used to house the private rooms. In this and the house next door, the *Museo del Ambiente Histórico* shows

tion between the lower town and Tivoli, the old quarter of the French immigrants, and leads straight to *Calle Jesús Rabi* and the *Museo de Lucha Clandestina* at the corner. The museum in the former police station is dedicated to the 26th of July Movement, commemorating the storm-

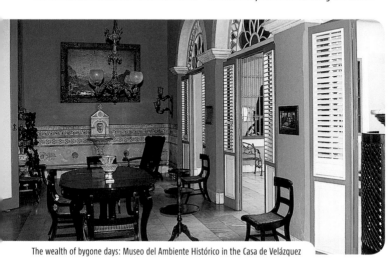

The wealth of bygone days: Museo del Ambiente Histórico in the Casa de Velázquez

furniture from the 16th to the 19th centuries. *C. Félix Peña 610 | Parque Céspedes | Mon–Sat 9am–4pm, Sun 9am–noon | Sun, Tue at 10am Peña de Danzón performance*

CEMENTERIO SANTA IFIGENIA
The focus of the cemetery is the grave of the poet and hero of the fight for freedom José Martí. This cemetery also holds the tomb of the Bacardí family. *Ave. Crombet | Mon–Fri 8am–6pm, Sat/Sun 8am–5pm | admission 1 CUC, photo/video permit 1/5 CUC*

ESCALINITA PADRE PICO/ CALLE JESÚS RABI
This pretty, wide set of steps flanked by houses is the most photogenic connec-

ing of the *Moncada* barracks *(Calle Jesús Rabi 1 | Tue–Sat 9am–7pm, Sun 9am–5pm | admission 1 CUC)*. During his studies in Santiago de Cuba, Fidel Castro lived at Calle Jesús Rabi 6.

LA MAQUETA
The entire city including its harbour bay as a model that fills a whole room – ideal to get an overview. Guides are at hand to explain the location and history of individual quarters. *Calle Corona 704 | betw. San Basilio/Santa Lucía | Tue–Sun 9am–9pm | admission 1 CUC*

INSIDER TIP ▶ MUSEO DEL CARNAVAL
Masks, costumes, typical musical instruments such as *congas* and *cornetas*, posters and photos give an idea of Santiago's

vibrant carnival (last week in July). *Heredia 303 | Tue–Sun 9am–5pm | folklore performances Tue–Sat 4pm, rumba show Sun 4pm (included in the admission fee) | 1 CUC*

MUSEO CASA DE LA TROVA ★ ●

A small stage, the walls full of photographs, a few seats for friends: the *Casa de la Trova* looked exactly like this before being turned into a small dance venue (now next door) for tourists. A fine homage to the original, estimated to be over 100 years old, where gifted singers und musicians perform bolero und son classics. If you want to support them, buy a CD. *Heredia 208 | daily 10am–6pm | free admission*

MUSEO HISTÓRICO 26 DE JULIO ●

Before the revolution, the *Moncada* barracks were the second-largest military quarters of Fulgencio Batista. Bullet holes serve as a reminder of Fidel Castro's failed coup of 26 July 1953. Today, the building houses a school and a *Revolution Museum (Ctra. Central/corner Gen. Portuondo | Mon–Sat 9am–5pm, Sun 9am–noon)*.

MUSEO PROVINCIAL EMILIO BACARDÍ

Adorned by columns, this temple of archaeology and city history was founded in 1899 as the first museum on Cuba. The writing desk of founder Emilio Bacardí Moreau stands at the entrance. *Pío Rosado/Aguilera | Tue–Sat 9am–9pm, Sun 9am–5pm | admission 2 CUC*

MUSEO DEL RON

If you've always wanted to find out how rum is produced, this museum will leave no question unanswered. A cellar bar awaits for tastings, a shop for your purchases. *Calle San Basilio 358 | daily 9am–9pm*

FOOD & DRINK

LAS GALLEGAS

This *paladar* might be worlds apart from its model restaurant in Havana, *La Guarida*, but the food is tasty: especially the lamb fricassee. *San Basilio 305 | tel. 022 62 47 00 | daily 1pm–midnight | Budget–Moderate*

GODS, CULTS & SAINTS

Similar to voodoo on Haiti and candomblé in Salvador de Bahía/Brazil, at ritual congregations of *santeros* priests on Cuba the *orishas*, around twenty good or bad deities, are invoked. This natural religion starts from the premise that every human being has been allocated at least one deity, Ochún, for instance, the goddess of vanity, Oyá, the dangerous goddess of vengeance, Yemayá, goddess of the sea and maternity, or Ogún, the womanizer, warrior and god of the mountains. For many Cubans it is completely normal to have various Afro-Cuban altars or shrines in the house. In the Spanish era, African gods were identified with Christian saints; in this way, these deities survived despite the inquisitorial pressure by the Church. The most widespread Afro-Cuban faith in Cuba is the Santería religion.

PALADAR SALÓN TROPICAL

Here you'll be served Cuban, Italian, and grilled delicacies cooked by expert hands and served on a lovely roof terrace. *Fernández Marcané 310 | Santa Bárbara | daily 1pm–midnight | tel. 022 64 11 61 | Budget*

SALÓN 1900

Dine by the light of chandeliers in one of the former residences of the Bacardí rum dynasty. The *sopa de mariscos* (seafood soup) is particularly good. *San Basílico | betw. San Félix/Carnicería | tel. 022 62 35 07 | daily 7–10am, noon–midnight, closed Tue | Budget*

ZÚNZUN

Feast in style either in the rooms or on the terrace of a villa. Large selection of tasty dishes, including Cuban specialities and seafood. *Ave. Manduley 159/Calle 7 | Vista Alegre | tel. 022 64 01 75 | daily noon–11pm | Budget–Expensive*

SHOPPING

CASA DEL HABANO

Large selection of cigars for lovers of world-class smokes. The shop belongs to the local tobacco factory. *Ave. Jesús Menéndez 703 | daily 9am–6pm | admission ticket for visit (5 CUC) from Cubatur at the cathedral*

LA MAISON

So what are Cuban women wearing this season? At Cuba's fashion store the prettiest girls of Santiago present creative Cuban style. The shop sells jewellery, souvenirs and leisure clothing too. Tickets for the fashion shows (*5 CUC*) can only be bought on the evening. *Ave. Manduley 52 | Vista Alegre | tel. 022 64 11 17*

ENTERTAINMENT

CABARET TROPICANA

Like the city as a whole, the famous revue is also a bit more easy-going than its equivalent in Havana. If the hot rhythms inspire you, why not follow up the show with a little boogie yourself in the club next door. *Km 1.5 | Autopista Nacional | tel. 022 68 70 20 | Fri/Sat from 10pm | admission 30 CUC*

CASA DE LA TROVA ●

Since the *Museo Casa de la Trova* was established in the building, the rooms behind and above have been reserved for the dancing crowd. *Heredia 208 | downstairs daily until 10pm (admission 1 CUC), afterwards upstairs, admission between 1 and 5 CUC*

PATIO DE LOS ABUELOS

Nearly every evening there is live music and dance in the courtyard in a friendly inclusive atmosphere. *Calle Pérez Carbó 5 | opposite Plaza de Marte | daily 9.30pm–2am*

PATIO ARTEX SANDUNGA

Here, the high jinks start in the morning – half of Santiago meets here for a lemonade or beer. There are souvenirs for sale, and a restaurant too. Daily live music. *Calle Heredia 304 | daily 9am–midnight | admission (if there are concerts on) 3 CUC*

WHERE TO STAY

LAS AMÉRICAS

This mid-range hotel is opposite the big *Santiago de Cuba* hotel. This has the advantage that you can use its shops and telephone. *70 rooms | Ave. Las Américas | tel. 022 64 20 11 | www.islazul.cu | Moderate*

INSIDER TIP ▶ **CASA EL TIVOLI**

Owners Sr. Luis Antonio Félix ('Luisito') and his wife Denia will receive you well. *Calle Rabi 107.5 | betw. Princesa and Santa Rosa | tel. 022 65 28 31 | lantoniofr@gmail.com | Budget*

CASA GRANDA

Splendidly restored former grand hotel. From the terrace you have a view across the entire *Parque Céspedes*, and the *Casa de la Trova* is just around the corner. *58 rooms, 3 suites | Parque Céspedes | tel. 022 65 30 21 (-24) | www.grancaribe.com | Moderate*

DOÑA MARÍA ELENA PONCE FAVERO

Private residence furnished with fabulous antiques. The hospitable hosts rent out 2 private rooms (both with bathroom, air-conditioning and fridge). *San Félix (Hartmann) no. 213 | betw. Maceo/San Mateo | tel. 022 65 12 97 | Budget*

MELIÁ SANTIAGO DE CUBA

The hotel in the city. Tennis courts, gym and a Jacuzzi pool are amongst the creature comforts within the glass, steel and concrete building. For shows and dances, you have the *Café Santiago*. *324 rooms | Ave. Las Américas/Calle M | tel. 022 68 70 70 | www.solmeliacuba.com | Expensive*

INFORMATION

CUBATUR

Tickets for a visit to the tobacco factory, reservations for daytrips, travel tips. *Parque Céspedes (opposite Casa Granda) | tel. 022 68 60 33 | daily 8.30am–5pm*

WHERE TO GO

BAYAMO (126 B4) (*Ⓜ M6*)

The capital (pop. 224,000) of the province of 'Granma' (named after the yacht on which the rebels landed on the western coast of this province in 1956) lies about 100km/60mi west of Santiago de Cuba. Not least a good base for trips to the west coast or into the Sierra Maestra national park, the city of Bayamo is also of great historical interest. On the main

Expect to hear the finest Cuban sounds In the Casa de la Trova

square, *Plaza de la Revolución,* visit the birthplace of Carlos Manuel Céspedes (1819–74), who issued the first declaration of independence in Bayamo. When the Spanish forces were nearing the city,

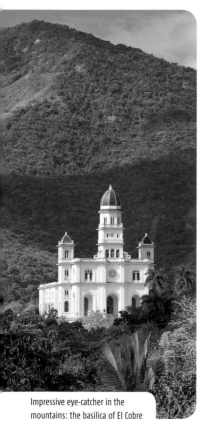

Impressive eye-catcher in the mountains: the basilica of El Cobre

its inhabitants set fire to their town rather than leave it to the Spanish. One of the places documenting this story is Céspedes' birth place *(Maceo no. 57 | Mon–Sat 8am–16pm, Sun 9am–1pm).* On the Plaza de la Revolución you'll also find the Islazul Hotel *Royalton (33 rooms | tel. 023 42 22 90 | Budget).* The biggest draw is

● **INSIDER TIP** Cerarte, Cuba's only waxworks. Look out for figures of musicians Benny Moré and Compay Segundo, Carlos Manuel de Céspedes and Ernesto Che Guevara *(Calle General García 221 | betw. Masó/Lora | Mon–Fri 9am–1pm, 2–5pm, Sun 6–10pm | free admission).*

EL COBRE (126 C5) (*N6*)
This small pilgrimage site, at the same time the centre of copper mining, lies a 20-minute drive from Santiago de Cuba in the mountains beyond Melgarejo. The white basilica (1927) crowning the green hill can be seen from afar. Inside the patron saint of Cuba, the *Virgen de la Caridad*, is enthroned above the altar. The car park has a view of the spoil heaps belonging to the copper mines.

LA COMANDANCIA DE LA PLATA ★
(126 B5) (*M6*)
A hike to the *Comandancia de La Plata* leads back to the beginnings of the revolution and into the national park surrounding Cuba's highest peak, *Pico Turquino* (1974m/6476ft) in the Sierra Maestra. The best starting point for the five-hour hike *(11 CUC incl. guide)* is the mountain village of *Santo Domingo* (73km/45mi southwest of Bayamo). In order to start off nice and early in the morning, you're best off spending the night before at the ⏱ *Villa Santo Domingo* hotel *(20 rooms | Ctra. La Plata, km 16 | tel. 023 56 56 35 | Budget),* built according to ecological guidelines. The *Comandancia de Ejército Rebelde* of La Plata served as a hiding place for the revolutionaries around Fidel Castro following their landing from Mexico to prepare the revolution. The first thing you see is the clearing where Castro landed in 1976 by helicopter. Then you can discover other buildings, 16 in total, some of them widely scattered on the

estate. Amongst them discover the field hospital where Che looked after the injured, Fidel Castro's *Casa Comandante* and the 'Palace of Justice', where justice was dispensed. A model in the adjoining museum shows the whole extent of the compound at a glance.

PARQUE DE BACONAO
(127 D5) (*∅ O6*)

Declared a biosphere reserve by Unesco, this park is the biggest leisure park on Cuba. The most beautiful beach is served by the *Hotel Bucanero (200 rooms | Ctra. Baconao, km 4 | tel. 022 68 63 63 | www. gran-caribe.com | Moderate)* – for 15 CUC per person, day guests are welcome here too. The 'Prehistoric Valley' *(Ctra. Baconao, km 9.5)* has been fitted out with natural-looking reproductions of dinosaurs and other prehistoric creatures *(see Travel with Children)*. Under a mile further on, car lovers will appreciate the *Museo Nacional del Transporte Terrestre*: the 44 vintage cars on display here include the Ford driven by Fidel Castro's mother Lina Ruz. A small building shows over 2000 miniature model cars *(Ctra. Baconao, km 8.5 | daily 8am–5pm | admission 1 CUC)*. At the kilometre 27.5 mark on Ctra. Baconao, the *Acuario Baconao (Tue–Sat 9am–5pm | admission from 7 CUC)* draws visitors thanks to its INSIDER TIP acrylic tunnel in the shark basin.

The greater part of the Baconao Park is taken up by the Cordillera Gran Piedra, boasting a gigantic rock, the *Gran Piedra* (1234m/4048ft), as its highest elevation. There is a ☀ mirador (viewpoint) with restaurant. Along the access road you'll find the *Hotel Gran Piedra (22 rooms | tel. 022 68 61 47 | Budget)* and the interesting *La Isabelica* coffee museum *(daily 8am–4pm | admission 1 CUC)* in an old coffee finca. *Ctra. Gran Piedra, km 14/ Ctra. Baconao*

PARQUE HISTÓRICO EL MORRO ☀
(126 C5) (*∅ N6*)

The well-preserved fort, designed in 1590 by Battista Antonelli, guards the entrance to the bay. The museum documents the sea battle between Spain and the USA. *Ctra. Del Morro | daily 8.30am–7.30pm | admission 4 CUC*

PILÓN/PLAYA MAREA DEL PORTILLO
(126 A5) (*∅ L6*)

The coastal road west of Santiago de Cuba is amongst the most scenically beautiful stretches in Cuba; it is, however, in a bad state of repair. Continually hugging a dramatic coast lined by bays, it leads (at Pilón) to the new tourist region on the Playa Marea del Portillo. West of Pilón marks the start of the *Parque Nacional Desembarco del Granma* (national park honouring the landing of the Granma). For its high number of endemic plants and animals, the park was included on the World Heritage Unesco list in 1999. It extends to the *Playa Las Coloradas,* where in 1956 Fidel Castro and his men arrived on the Granma from exile in Mexico.

LOW BUDGET

▶ Take the horse-drawn carriage through Holguín or Bayamo, the town of the carriages – probably the most charming way to save effort and money on the road! A ride only costs 2–3 CUC.

▶ On Sunday and Thursday at 10am, visiting the *Casa de Velázquez* in Santiago de Cuba is worth your while twice over, as a *Peña de Danzón* (dance & music) performance takes place at that time and is included in the admission price.

TRIPS & TOURS

The tours are marked in green in the road atlas,
the pull-out map and on the back cover

① THE GREEN WEST: ORCHIDS, CAVES, FERTILE SOIL

Starting from Havana, this round trip some 400km/ 250 mi long leads you to the oldest part of the island, geologically speaking: the waters of the densely wooded Sierra del Rosario, in the tobacco town of Pinar del Río and its fertile hinterland with the beautiful Valle de Viñales and its mogotes, primeval lime mountains. Try to pencil in two overnight stays before driving back.

Leave the capital Havana → p. 32 by taking Avenida 5 (Miramar), then Calle 146a (first turn-off left past the exit to Centro de las Convenciones) and Calle 23 (take a right at the first roundabout) as the most direct way to reach the motorway *(autopista)* to Pinar del Río. At km 65 of autopista A 4 (at the petrol station) you have reached the exit to Soroa → p. 53, which is situated only a few minutes by car from the motorway on the slope of the densely forested Sierra del Rosario: discover its splendid, richly endowed orchid garden, the *El Salto* waterfall, over 30m/100ft high, and the *Hotel Soroa*. Nearby you'll also find the picturesque mountain lake and the good *Hotel Moka* that are part of the ecotourism complex Las Terrazas → p. 54.

Afterwards, get back onto the motorway and drive on to the lively provincial capital of Pinar del Río → p. 51, the centre of local tobacco region. You'll find quiet

Photo: Valle de Viñales at Pinar del Río

An adventure by rental car through the country or a ride on the historical electric train through the sugar-cane fields

and well-kept accommodation in the *Casa de Elena Rabelo*, while the *Paladar El Mesón* will spoil you with generous portions → p. 52. You may of course keep a visit to the town with its pretty houses – on Calle Martí, in particular – for the drive back. Continue into the Valle de Viñales → p. 54, 53km/33mi away. At the edge of Viñales town on the rural road you'll reach the El Palenque de los Cimarrones cave and the Cueva del Indio → p. 54, 100. A good place to stay in style – with a view

of the famous limestone mountains called mogotes – is INSIDER TIP *Casa Tito Crespo (Las Maravillas 58 | tel. 048 79 33 83 | Budget)*. The bungalow is surrounded by a pretty tropical garden. If you want to go for a swim, make sure to reserve at least one day to visit the pretty beaches of the uninhabited beach island of Cayo Jutías → p. 55 at Santa Lucía (40km/25mi northwest of Viñales and reached via a causeway), before returning to Havana.

2 TAKE THE OLD STEAM TRAIN TO HERSHEY

If you'd rather not drive yourself, you can join organised trips, for example from Havana by bus to Guanabo and from there on the nostalgic Hershey Express *(www.transhershey.com)* through sugar-cane fields to the former sugar village of Hershey. Plenty of fun and entertainment are thrown in too. The trip takes a good 6 hours and costs 80 euros per person including lunch with locally available drinks.

In the morning, the operator *(Cuba Real Tours → p. 43)* picks up all participants and starts off by taking them to the other side of the *Bahía de la Habana* to the hill bearing the statue of Christ, which yields the best view of the Old Town. In an ironic touch of history it was erected by the wife of the last dictator Fulgencio Batista, in thanks for the fact that her husband had survived an assassination attempt; the 17m/55ft-high marble figure created by Cuban sculptor Jilma Madera was completed only a few days before Batista's flight: on 25 December 1958.

The bus now takes the pretty Via Blanca coastal road to Guanabo (approx. 26km/16mi east of Havana), which is considered the last amongst the towns along the Playas del Este → p. 48 (not counting the *Playa Jibacoa* further away). At the small inconspicuous train

Welcome in style on the railway line to Hershey

station of Guanabo everybody changes from the bus to the red wagons of the *Hershey Express* and is welcomed by the Cuban 'Los Brill' sextet and its dancers. *Brill* was also the name of the electric rail cars brought over in the mid-1920s from the US to Cuba by chocolate king Milton Hershey (1857–1945), to transport workers from Havana to Hershey's sugar-cane fields and sugar factories in the province of Matanzas. For eighty years, his train was the only electric train in Cuba and in fact the only means of transport to the northern coast. The journey takes about 90 minutes in total, going past a few cattle pastures with tall royal palms, the scattered shade-givers typical for Cuba, and soon leads right through wide sugar-cane fields. During a short stop the guide tells of a mistake made by the Cubans after the fall of sugar prices on the world market: not to have waited calmly for developments. 'Today, cultivation would be viable again,' he says, 'but too many sugar factories have since been abandoned.' The train continuing full steam ahead, rum is served, and INSIDER TIP the band gets a party atmosphere going. How about a little dance? A photo with a conductor's cap on your head, hands on the brake lever and on the accelerator crank, one foot on the horn? This way the journey time until arrival at Central Hershey (*Central* is the Cuban name for the sugar factories) passes in a flash.

Finished in 1918, Central Hershey was nationalised following the revolution and abandoned in 2002, yet on a walk around you still get a good idea of the progressive layout of the factory village. The most important shops are lined up along the main road; there's a pharmacy, a school, a church, sports facilities und cottages for the workers. They were well looked after here – in contrast to other pre-revolutionary sugar factories. Today however, unemployment rules.

There are many impressions in visitors' minds to discuss during lunch afterwards in the nearby *Centro recreativo*, a beautiful park with a small lake and ancient trees. After lunch, it's back on the bus to Havana (or Varadero).

3 TO THE CAYOS AND PLAYAS OF THE NORTH

This route of approx. 300km/190mi is ideal for the curious who would like to take a look at the neighbouring holiday paradise too. If you are based on Cayo Coco or on Cayo Guillermo, visit Playa Santa Lucía or vice versa.

Let's assume you are holidaying in Playa Santa Lucía → p. 65 in the eastern part of Cuba's northern coast. Reserve for the next two nights a hotel in the *Motel Jardín los Cocos* on Cayo Coco (*24 rooms | Carretera a Cayo Paredón Grande | Ensenada Bautista | tel. 033 30 81 31, 033 30 81 21 | www.islazul.cu | Moderate*), so you don't end up without accommodation at your destination. And don't forget to bring your passport, you'll need it to cross over to Cayo Coco on the causeway. In order to then get from Playa Santa Lucía to Cayo Coco or Cayo Guillermo, you'll leave the holiday resort via the only exit road, leading southwest towards Camagüey. First you'll be driving through the green plain of the rivers Rosalia, Molina and Najarro, before the countryside starts to rise gently at the *Parador Santa Isabel*. After some 80km/50mi you've already reached Camagüey → p. 63, the charming capital of the province. At the Plaza San Juan de Dios, fringed by pretty colonial buildings, friendly patio restaurants await your custom. Have a break here before the one-hour drive to Ciego

de Ávila → p. 69. This tranquil centre of cattle raising doesn't offer any great sights, however, so turn off right before reaching the town and take the road towards Morón, and soon you'll enjoy the pretty, open pasture country of the coastal floodplain.

After about half an hour's drive already you reach Morón → p. 70, the last sizeable settlement before the cayos in the north. Shortly before the roundabout turn off right to Cayo Coco. After another stretch of about twenty minutes, you've quickly reached the barrier for the Pedraplén, the 16km/10mi-long causeway leading to Cayo Coco → p. 68. Here you have to provide documentary proof (passport) that you are a tourist and pay a 2 CUC toll per person (the same applies on the way back).

During the drive across you will see flocks of pink flamingos. At the information stand, prettily roofed with palm leaves, you can buy a map with the layout of the hotels on the island, to make it easier to find the freely accessible beaches. The prettiest beach lies at the very end of Cayo Guillermo, which is also connected with Cayo Coco by a drivable causeway: INSIDER TIP *Playa Pilar* (with restaurant). Another attraction, apart from the incredibly clear water and powder-like white sandy beach, is a catamaran trip to the offshore island of Media Luna (5 CUC) as well as a diving trip to the colourful coral reef (another additional 3 CUC); a beach deckchair costs 1 CUC per day.

For the same tour in the other direction – i.e. if your holiday base is on Cayo Coco – the best thing to do is to reserve a room in the reasonably priced *Escuela Santa Lucía* hotel (*31 rooms | Playa | tel. 032 33 63 10 | Budget*), in Playa Santa Lucía, and follow the above itinerary the other way round.

WHERE IT ALL BEGAN: ROUND TRIP FROM GUARDALAVACA ON THE REVOLUTION TRAIL

This route, about 450km/280mi long, with overnight stays in Santiago de Cuba and Baracoa, leads you via Bayamo, Moa and the Bahía de Nipe back to Guardalavaca. This is a tour to the beginnings of the revolution and Spanish colonisation, but most of all it's a scenic treat.

Worth a visit, Holguín → p. 77 is so close to Guardalavaca → p. 79 that you are better off exploring it on a day trip rather than on this tour. So drive briskly on the ring road in the direction of Santiago, which leads you 71km/44mi through the plain on the edge of the Sierra Maestra, southwest through foothills of the Sierra, down to Bayamo → p. 85. Founded as early as 1513 by Diego de Velázquez, this town displays a nice healthy confidence, and has good small hotels and many private accommodation options. By virtue of its central position between the scenic but not yet touristy Gulf of Guacanayabo, the Sierra Maestra and the river plain of the Río Cauto it is one of the cities in Cuba with a great potential for the future. From here you can take trips on the trail of the revolution, e. g. via Bartolomé Masó to Santo Domingo (79km/49 mi) and from there on foot into the Sierra Maestra to the former rebel camp of La Comandancia de La Plata → p. 86. For this detour reckon on a night in Santo Domingo; on the afternoon of the following day then you can drive back to Bayamo at leisure and from there via Contramaestre and Palma Soriano on to Santiago (128km/79mi).

Plan at least one day and one overnight stay for Santiago de Cuba → p. 80: who wouldn't want to have a boogie in the legendary *Casa de la Trova* or at

least listen to the best of Cuban's bolero singers or son musicians at the *Museo Casa de la Trova*? The *El Morro* fortress is another must-see – being one of the last still standing of those erected by the Spanish to guard against English pirate attacks in the Caribbean Sea. You should be well rested for the next leg to Baracoa (234km/145mi) in the farthest east of Cuba. You leave Santiago de Cuba on the A1, turn off after a few miles to the country road towards El Cristo, Alto Songo and La Maya and reach the motorway leading to Guantánamo; once on that, follow the signs for Baracoa. After some 25km/15mi you will pass the access road to the Mirador de Los Malones (currently closed), from which you used to be able to see the US military base, and after a drive of some 48km/30mi along the Caribbean coast reach *Farola*,

the bendy pass road through the mountains to Baracoa → p. 75. In this small town with a cosy feel, once Cuba's first colonial settlement, many good-value private accommodation options are available if you want to stay longer.

The drive to Moa is one of Cuba's most scenic routes. Unfortunately, well over 65km/40mi of it are on dirt road, so you can only drive at about 40kmh/25mph. Stunning bays, river estuaries and the tranquillity of the landscape do their best to compensate. From Moa, the road is good again, and you'll make faster progress through a landscape of green conical mountains along the Bahía de Nipe to the exit for Cayo Saetía → p. 79. Those not averse to another stretch of bad road (Guaro–Herrera) can drive back to Guardelavaca via Banes or else take the road via Holguín.

Baracoa, a tranquil little colonial town in the mountains

SPORTS & ACTIVITIES

Cuba has adapted to the sporting needs of its visitors. Well-equipped marinas, the bases of catamarans and motorboats for fishing and pleasure trips, line the coasts. The national parks are criss-crossed by senderos (hiking trails).

State-run travel agencies run excursions on foot, on horseback or by bike, in the national parks trekking and birdwatching too. Golfers appreciate Varadero's 18-hole course, up to now the only one of its kind, although more are being planned, e.g. on the Costa Esmeralda. Tennis players can get active on the many hotel courts. Most of all though Cuba offers fantastic diving sites.

BIKING

In Cuba, where the pushbike is still the basic means of transport for many, you'll always have some company – one of the reasons why bike tours are so much fun. Longer tours are better booked in advance back home with a specialised operator (see p. 111).

BIRDWATCHING

Passionate birdwatchers can expect 338 species of birds, amongst them 24 of the 58 Caribbean species, including 20 endemics that can only be found on Cuba. Good stalking grounds include the national parks La Güira and Ciénaga de Zapata, also Cayo Coco and Topes de

Fans of water sports and nature world can look forward to sheer paradise in beach resorts and mountains or between 1001 islands

Collantes (bookings through *Cubatur* or *EcoTur* | *www.ecoturcuba.co.cu*); bird-watching tours are also on offer through the specialist operator Geodyssey *(www. geodyssey.co.uk)*.

Artex | *5ta Ave. Nr. 8010/82* | *Miramar, Playa* | *tel. 07 204 27 10* | *www.artexsa. com)*. Also on offer are workshops on movements, rites and songs of Cuban Santería (dance course from 150 CUC).

DANCING

If you want to learn how to dance Cuban son, cha-cha-cha or salsa, you can book classes back home with a specialised operator *(see chapter 'Travel Tips')* or on the island, e. g. in Havana at *DARTE (División*

DIVING

Cuba's ⭐ *diving sites* around the island are in a class of their own. This is an overview of the best spots:
Cayo Largo: caves and drop-offs with almost 600 coral species and hundreds of

species of sponges. You'll find a diving school at Playa Sirena.

Faro Luna/Cienfuegos: a highlight are the many underwater canyons in the immediate vicinity of the diving basis.

Guardalavaca/Playas Esmeralda/Pesquero: diving in depths of 5–40m/15–130ft near the Bahamas Channel. Everywhere you look: caves, grottoes and coral valleys.

Isla de la Juventud: the area with the most diving spots on Cuba (56) lies between 13 and 20 nautical miles from Hotel Colony.

Jardines del Rey: coral gardens with soft and hard coral, grottoes, caves, canyons, crevasses and wrecks, all in crystal-clear waters (visibility up to 40m/130ft) with an unusual abundance of fish, including awe-inducing whale sharks: a true paradise for (experienced) reef divers.

Marea del Portillo: diving and snorkelling area with 16 spots, amongst them entire forests of the rare black coral.

María La Gorda: the diving sites close to the coast (between 15 and 30 minutes by boat) lie at the outside reef, which drops down to depths of 2500m/8000ft. Due to the weak currents these are good grounds for beginners too. Visibility often over 40m/130ft!

Playa Santa Lucía: particularly high numbers of fish appear between November and May; however, outside those months the sea is calmer. One attraction is **INSIDER TIP** feeding the sharks (bull sharks).

Santiago de Cuba: over 23 diving spots with wonderful tunnels, steep rock walls and coral mountains.

Varadero: coral reefs, caves and wrecks – all in all 30 diving spots await you all around the beach peninsula and its large tourist hotels.

A big draw for experienced divers: wreck diving

Prices: a dive starts at 30 CUC, hire gear at 10 CUC and a course costs between 129 and 330 CUC. For a few CUC, snorkellers may hire flippers and diving masks at several public swimming beaches by the hour, e. g. on Cayo Jutiás and at Playa Pilar on Cayo Guillermo.

For a comprehensive programme of diving trips to Cuba, contact *Regal Dive (tel. 01353 65 99 99 | www.regal-diving. co.uk).*

FISHING

The abundance of fish in the Florida Strait is legendary. The best seasons for amateur anglers are the months of May to December. Trips take between 4 and 8 hours and cost between 280 and 540 CUC. They are offered in the well-equipped marinas, e. g. in Havana's *Marina Hemingway,* in the *Marina Tarara* (Playas del Este), the *Marina Cayo Guillermo* as well as in the south in the *Marinas Cienfuegos* and *Cayo Largo.* For more information see *www.nauticamarlin.com.* Freshwater anglers meet – outside the close season in June – on the Laguna de Leche near Morón, or on the Zaza and Hanabanilla reservoir lakes. The licence costs 20 CUC. Booking through the Cubatur travel agencies.

GOLF

The 18-hole golf course (72 par) of Varadero *(Varadero Golf Club | Ave. Las Américas | tel. 045 66 73 88 | www.varadero-golfclub.com)* boasts a beautiful location, extending in the east of the peninsula between the Las Morlas beach road and the Avenida Las Américas on the lagoon. Playing 18 holes costs 70 CUC, 9 holes 48 CUC. There is also the *Golfito* or *Diplo-Golf,* a 9-hole golf course laid out in 1920 by homesick British expatriates *(Capdevila,* *Boyeros | tel. 07 845 45 78 | green fee 20 CUC),* which also accepts visiting players. Lying approx. 13km/8mi from Vedado, it is also called 'El Golfito'.

SAILING

Marinas with moorings or opportunities to hire boats are available for instance in Havana, Varadero and Cienfuegos *(check www.nauticamarlin.com | www.gaviota-grupo.com).* Entering by sea the crew has to contact the harbour authorities even before reaching sovereign waters (twelve nautical miles). For this, you have to use either the HF channels (SSB) 2760 (National Coastal Network) and 2790 (Tourism Network) or the VHF channels 68 for the National Coastal Network and 16 for the Tourism Network. Helpful literature: Cuba – A Cruising Guide.

TREKKING

Hike up to the summit of the Pico Turquino or explore the Humboldt National Park, and walk through the forests around Topes de Collantes or Las Terrazas ... However, don't walk on your own, but only with a group. In the national parks, you even have to be accompanied by a state-licensed guide (registration and booking through the local information centres or agencies). For more information, talk to *EcoTur (www.ecoturcuba. co.cu).*

WINDSURFING

Windsurfers find good to excellent wind conditions at the beaches of Guardalavaca, Playa Santa Lucía and Varadero (on average 2–6 Beaufort). All-inclusive hotels with a sizeable sports programme offer introductory courses and provide hire gear.

TRAVEL WITH KIDS

On Cuba, you'll see large posters stating confidently that '200 million children will be sleeping on the streets tonight. None of them will be Cuban.' A proud statement which – propaganda or no propaganda – makes one thing clear: no matter what their origin and skin colour, all children are looked after here.

If you know Latin America a little, you'll know that Cuba is the subcontinent's most progressive country in this respect. Travelling with your family you'll encounter a seriousness in dealing with children that goes far beyond sentimental love. Nearly all leisure activities include some educational aspects. For Europeans and North Americans this is not unusual – you'll feel at home. There's only one

thing here where Cuba is very different: the lack of toys has to be compensated by imagination. But that isn't such a bad thing surely – maybe it's even a good remedy for the consumer pressures ruling children's lives at home.

HAVANA

ACUARIO DEL CENTRO HISTÓRICO
(122 A2) (*☉ D2*)

For fans of the primeval: a manjuarí fish guards the entrance to this aquarium with its mystical lighting. This species has been around for a near-unimaginable length of time: 130 million years! *Calle Teniente Rey | betw. Oficios/Mercaderes | Tue–Sat 9am–5pm, Sun 9am–1pm | admission 1 CUC, children up to 12 free*

Photo: Family scene in Parque Cespedes, Santiago de Cuba

Lions at the car window, Indians, dinos and crocs, cave adventures – and again and again, 'Flipper' in action

ACUARIO NACIONAL (122 A2) *(⪥ D2)*
Big water fun park featuring of course 'Flipper' (well, dolphins, anyway), bursting into action at showtime. *Ave. 3ra/62 | Miramar | Tue–Sun 10am–5.30pm | admission 7, children 5 CUC*

JARDÍN ZOO DE LA HABANA
(122 A2) *(⪥ D2)*
Round trips on the miniature train or a horse-drawn carriage, playground, pony riding, a museum and of course real animals too, including lions, zebras, chimps

and hippos; in Havana's old zoo there is no shortage of entertainment for the young ones. *Ave. 26/Ave. del Zoológico | Tue–Sun 9am–5.30pm | admission 2, children up to 12 years of age 1 CUC*

LA BOCA/GUAMÁ (122 B–C3) *(⪥ E–F3)*
On the crocodile farm in La Boca, crocodile tamer Chacón shows off the scars on his legs and arms, not without a certain pride *(daily 8am–4.30pm | admission 5*

Beyond the entrance there are real dolphins: Varadero's Delfinario

CUC). And children will love the 32 life-like sculptures of Indians by Rita Longa in Guamá. *Departures in La Boca | 10 CUC, children 5 CUC | Peninsula de Zapata*

BOAT TRIP ON THE RÍO CANIMAR
(122 C2) (*ω F2*)

Every day at noon, at the *Parque Turístico Canimar* below the bridge (signposted), a boat departs for a 45-min trip on the Río Canimar to the shore ranch of *La Arboleda*. After having lunch there, you're free to go on a horseback hack or trip in a rowing boat, until it's time to head back, at 4.30pm. *Ctra. Varadero–Matanzas | tel. 045 26 15 16 | adults 25, children 12.50 CUC*

CUEVA DEL INDIO (120 C3) (*ω C2*)

A true cave adventure: first 250m/275yd into the mountain on foot, then on by boat, and out again the other side. *Valle de Viñales | daily 9am–6pm | 5 CUC, children up to the age of 10 go free*

CUEVAS DE BELLAMAR ● (122 B2) (*ω E2*)

The adventurous will enjoy this more than the usual guided tour through the accessible parts of the cave: the INSIDER TIP Tour de la Esponja through unlit areas. The only light comes from a headtorch. *Ctra. a la Cuevas, Matanzas | daily 9am–5pm | admission 5 CUC, Tour de la Esponja 8, children up to 12 years of age 6 CUC*

DELFINARIO (122 C2) (*ω F2*)

Nearly a dozen dolphins delight children and adults with their artistry and approachability. *Autopista Sur, km 14 | Varadero | admission incl. show (11am, 3, 5pm) 15 CUC, swimming with dolphins (9.30am, 3.30pm) 89 CUC*

MUSEO PROVINCIAL
(122 B2) (*ω E2*)

One attraction has to be observed under the magnifying glass: INSIDER TIP two preserved fleas that have been dressed in clothes. Before you get to them, there's a 130-year old mummy too. *Milanés/Magdalena | Matanzas | Tue–Sat 9.30am–noon and 1–5pm, Sun 9am–noon | admission 2 CUC*

THE CENTRE

JUNGLE TOUR (124 C1) (⍾ J2–3)

An exploration of the mangrove maze of Cayo Guillermo by motorboat is not only exciting for children, the parents too will enjoy this a lot! *Marina Cayo Guillermo | adults 39, children 19.50 CUC*

MORÓN CALEIDOSCOPE
(124 C2) (⍾ J3)

By steam train through sugar-cane fields, by horse-drawn carriage through Morón and by boat on to the Laguna de Leche: a day trip that will stay in everybody's minds for a long time. A highlight is the crocodile farm of *La Rosa*. *Reservations in the hotels or tel. 033 30 12 15 | adults 65, children 48.75 CUC*

PARQUE NATURAL EL BAGÁ
(124 C1) (⍾ K3)

The most exciting way to explore the park is on horseback. You'll see many animals, including iguanas and croco-diles. *Cayo Coco | Mon–Sat 9.30am–4.30pm | admission from 10, children from 5 CUC*

THE EAST

ACUARIO CAYO NARANJO
(126 C3) (⍾ N4–5)

The fun starts with the crossing, as the basins for the dolphins and other sea creatures lie on an island in Naranjo Bay. *Ctra. Guardalavaca, km 48 | daily 9am–4.30 | admission incl. boat transfer 42, children 21 CUC, 100 / 50 CUC incl. swimming with dolphins*

ALDEA TAÍNA (126 C3) (⍾ N5)

With war paint, loincloths and headbands around their long black hair, these 'Indi-ans' look pretty authentic; their job is to perform their dances for groups (of at least 10). Ask at the hotel whether enough people are interested. *Ctra. a Banes | daily 9am–4pm | admission to village 3 CUC*

VALLE DE LA PREHISTORIA
(127 D5) (⍾ O5)

Mammoths, sabre-tooth tigers, tyran-nosaurus rex – in this pre-historic valley, dino fans won't know where to look first. All 227 figures are life-size. *Ctra. a Bacon-ao, km 6.5 | daily 8am–5pm | admission 1, children 0.50 CUC*

Life-size: figures of Indians in the Aldea Taína

FESTIVALS & EVENTS

Cuba parties more thoroughly than many of its Caribbean neighbours, and often with a high artistic standard. The various festivals in particular have an excellent international reputation, most of all the *Festival Internacional del Nuevo Cine Latinoamericano,* the International Festival of New Latin American film in Havana, which takes place in December with a large number of representatives from nearly all Latin American countries. Other festivals have placed Cuba once again at the heart of the Caribbean in cultural terms. In Havana, this includes the international guitar contest held every other year and the International Benny Moré Festival for popular music in Cienfuegos. But the annual award of the Cuban literary prize, the International Jazz Festival and the Biennial of Fine Arts in Havana get a lot of attention too. For up-to-date information on the cultural scene see: *www.travel2cuba.co.uk* and *www.cubaabsolutely.com.*

HOLIDAYS

1 Jan *Día de la Liberación* (Liberation Day); **8 March** *International Women's Day;* **1 May** *Labour Day*; **26 July** *Día de la Rebeldía Nacional* (Day of the Storming of the Moncada Barracks); **10 Oct** *Aniversario del comienzo de la primera Guerra de Independencia* (commemoration of the start of the first War of Independence); **25 Dec** *Navidad* (Christmas)

EVENTS

DECEMBER/JANUARY
▶ *Feria Internacional de Artesanía* in Havana: major crafts fair with exhibitors from all over the world, in particular from Latin America and the Caribbean

FEBRUARY
▶ *Fiesta de las Toronjas:* grapefruit harvest on the Isla de La Juventud, where rivers of *guachi* (grapefruit firewater) flow

MARCH
▶ *Benny Moré Music Festival* (varying dates) in Cienfuegos

APRIL
▶ *Semana de la Cultura:* arts week in Baracoa with children's carnival

MAY
▶ *Torneo Internacional de la Pesca de la Aguja 'Ernest Hemingway':* fishing competition at the Marina Hemingway

Not just any old fiestas – carnival and famous festivals add colour to the revolutionary calendar of events

in Havana (23–28); *rpublicas@prto. mh.cyt.cu*

JULY
▶ *Festival del Caribe:* music and dance groups heat things up in Santiago de Cuba; culminating at the end of the month in the ▶ ★ *Carnival* in Santiago, the hottest on the island

JULY/AUGUST
▶ *Carnival* in Havana: masks, floats, street and children's parties, live music, grandstands on the Malecón

AUGUST
▶ *Festival de Teatro de la Habana:* from late August; *www.fth.cult.cu*

SEPTEMBER
▶ *Torneo Internacional de la Pesca del Castero 'Blue Marlin':* fishing competition at the Marina Hemingway in Havana (19–24); *rpublicas@prto.mh.cyt.cu*

OCTOBER
▶ *Fiesta de la Cultura Iberoamericana:* readings, exhibitions, etc. in Holguín
▶ *International Ballet Festival* in Havana (last week in October)

NOVEMBER
▶ *Copa Varadero:* sailing regatta off Varadero

DECEMBER
▶ ★ *Festival Internacional del Nuevo Cine Latinoamericano:* International Festival of Latin American film in Havana; *www.habanafilmfestival.com*
▶ INSIDERTIP *Parrandas:* carnivalesque processions in Remedios (16 and 24)
▶ *Regatta Felíz Navidad:* the Christmas regatta from the Marina Hemingway to the El Morro fort makes the splendid finish to the year in the capital

LINKS, BLOGS, APPS & MORE

▶ www.traveltocubainfo.com Metasite listing sites with photographs, books, a link to solidarity campaigns and information on peaceful dissidents such as the Damas del Blanco

▶ http://www.biography.com/people/fidel-castro-9241487 Get past the ad, and find an in-depth exploration of Fidel Castro's biography

▶ www.cubarte.cult.cu Interested in the arts? If you have a smattering of Spanish, will find up-to-date information on current events. Also eminently helpful: the collection of links under *Portales Nacionales* and *Portales Provinciales*. Even Fidel Castro's *Reflexiones* are here.

▶ www.cubaabsolutely.com Nicely presented online magazine that goes beyond basic information for travellers by posting some in-depth features on Cuban society and history, on music and the arts scene.

▶ http://desdecuba.com/generationy/ Fascinating and comprehensive blog by a young female intellectual dissident on the very real limitations on women's lives on Cuba. Little known inside Cuba, where internet access is limited, Yoani Sanchez is one of the 'despicable parasites' recently denigrated by Mariela Castro, the president's daughter.

▶ http://www.cubaforums.com/ Tourist reviews, recommendations & discussions of Cuba's hotels, resorts, transport, culture and general travel advice

▶ www.vocescubanas.com Currently probably the most exciting platform: several Cuban intellectuals have provided their image or their logo for this blog made in Cuba. Also available as a free app through the iTunes App Store

Regardless of whether you are still preparing your trip or already in Cuba: these addresses will provide you with more information, videos and networks to make your holiday even more enjoyable

▶ http://vimeo.com/9896852 Very atmospheric video which places the focus on the inhabitants of Havana's Old Town and gives them a beautiful, poetically inspired stage. In only four minutes, this film (on youtube's arty brother Vimeo) manages to provide a deep insight into Cuban life; in HD quality

▶ http://video.nationalgeographic.com/video/kids/people-places-kids/cuba-photographer-kids/ A good eight-minute introduction to the island by National Geographic - although it's on the kids' page, this is very suitable for adults who want a first impression

▶ Cubilete 1.1.2 Traditional Cuban dice game for Android handsets, which may be played against three virtual adversaries. Every player throws the dice up to three times with the goal to achieve a set of five doublets of the maximum value

▶ Bongos A rhythm once started you can never stop: bongo percussions on the (Android) mobile create Cuba feeling everywhere

▶ Cuba Map by CITY APP Maps for Havana, Santiago de Cuba, Guantánamo, Holguín, Camagüey and Varadero with streets, restaurants, attractions – still leaving a bit to be desired, but you won't find a much better map even on paper. For iPhone and iPad

▶ http://www.lonelyplanet.com/thorntree/forum.jspa?forumID=14 The large *Lonely Planet* readership exchanges its views and tips on travelling to and in Cuba on the *Thorn Tree Travel Forum*. Up-to-date news and discussions

▶ www.twitter.com Thorny issue, after rumours of Fidel Castro's death appeared on the social networking site, the Cuban authorities are accusing Twitter of being pro-US.

▶ http://twitter.com/#!/CubaJunky Netherlands-based enthusiastic tweets on new restaurant openings etc.

TRAVEL TIPS

ARRIVAL

✈ International airlines such as Air France or Iberia usually only land in Havana and Varadero, while charter companies servicing the major package operators also fly to Cayo Coco and Holguín. Flights can be had from 630 £ (last-minute remaining seats for short stays) from London. At immigration, holidaymakers need to show a passport that is at least 6 months valid still and a tourist card (currently 18 £/ 29 US$). Individual travellers receive this from specialised operators (e.g. together with their flight booking) or by post from the Cuban embassy (cheque plus stamped return envelope). For package tourists this is usually included in the holiday price. When leaving the country, another 25 CUC has to be paid, and the copy of the tourist card handed back. Unless entering Cuba from a third country such as Canada, Mexico or the Bahamas, US citizens can only travel to Cuba with a licence issued by the Department of Treasury.

BUSES

The modern and air-conditioned buses of *Viazul* run between all cities on Cuba and are usually even on time. The journey from Havana to Varadero, for instance costs 10 CUC. Prices and routes are listed under *www.viazul.cu*. Address and bus station in Havana: *Ave. 26/Zoológico | tel. 07 8 811108*.

CAR HIRE

No international car rental firms are active on Cuba. If you want to book at good rates, talk to a specialised operator. For 5 days expect to pay 56 CUC/day. On the island insurance of at least 15 CUC/day is added. Drivers (at least 21 years of age) have to show a national licence, and their credit card will be swiped for 200 CUC or more as security. When you receive the car, check whether the spare wheel fits (if not, you might be asked to cough up at a later date for one that fits). There might be some small print in the contract requiring you to do an inspection every 10,000 km. Make sure that the next due inspection is marked in the contract. Should you reach the relevant number of kilometres, head for the nearest hire station to change the car. If you don't do this, you might have to pay a fine. The same applies for any oil changes that might be due. In the holiday centres you can hire scooters; in Varadero for instance from 12 (2 hrs) to 24 CUC (24 hrs, plus 40 £/ 65 US$ security).

RESPONSIBLE TRAVEL

It doesn't take a lot to be environmentally friendly whilst travelling. Don't just think about your carbon footprint whilst flying to and from your holiday destination but also about how you can protect nature and culture abroad. As a tourist it is especially important to respect nature, look out for local products, cycle instead of driving, save water and much more. If you would like to find out more about eco-tourism please visit: *www.ecotourism.org*

From arrival to weather

**From the start to the end of the holiday:
useful addresses and information for your trip to Cuba**

CLIMATE, WHEN TO GO

On Cuba the sun shines all year round. In the winter months (the dry season) the nights are colder than in summer, and a few days might be cold too. If you don't like high levels of humidity, visit in the dry season (mid-November to April). The other months are the rainy season. During that time hurricanes may sweep Cuba, in particular between late August and late October.

CONSULATES & EMBASSIES

EMBASSIES OF THE REPUBLIC OF CUBA (INTEREST SECTION IN THE US)
– 167 High Holborn | London WC1V 6PA | UK | tel. 0207 240 24 88 | embacuba@cubaldn.com | http://www.cubadiplomatica.cu/reinounido
– 2630 16th Street NW| Washington DC | 20009 | tel. 0202 797 85 18 20 | recepcion@sicuw.org | http://www.cubadiplomatica.cu/sicw

UK EMBASSY
Calle 34 No. 702e/7ma y 17 | Miramar, Playa | Habana | tel. 07 2 14 22 00 | http://ukincuba.fco.gov.uk/en/

US INTEREST SECTION
Calzada between L&M Streets | Vedado | Habana | tel. 07 833 3551 | havanaconsularinfo@state.gov | http://havana.usint.gov

CUSTOMS

Visitors may bring items for personal use into Cuba, but no electrical appliances. Radios, satellite telephones, and GPS systems too need an import licence. You may not export books that were published over 50 years ago in Cuba, crayfish, over 50 cigars or art – unless you have the requisite export permits with stamp. Information: www.aduana.co.cu. Entering Cuba from a EU country, you may bring 200 cigarettes or 100 cigarillos or 50 cigars or 250 g of tobacco; 1 l of spirits; or 2 l of alcoholic drinks no more than 22 % vol.; also goods with a value of up to 360 £. With the US, the situation is more complex, see http://www.aduana.co.cu/.

BUDGETING

Dance show	from 60 £/ 95 US$ e.g. at the Tropicana
Coffee	0.60–1.20 £/ 1.00–2.00 US$ for a cup
Water	0.60 £/ 1.00 US$ for a 1.5 l bottle (not cooled)
Chocolate	0.60 £/ 1.00 US$ 250 g from Baracoa
Petrol	0.85 £/ 1.35 US$ for a litre of super unleaded
Cocktail	from 2.5 £/ 4.00 US$ for a Cuba libre or mojito in a bar

DOMESTIC FLIGHTS

In order to get a seat on a domestic flight, you have to book at least two weeks ahead. The Havana–Santiago

de Cuba connection (800km/500mi as the crow flies) is particularly in demand; return tickets with Cubana or Aerocaribbean from 150 £/240 US$. The *Cubana de Aviación office is at: Calle Infanta/Humboldt | Vedado | Havana | tel. 0053 733 44 46 | www. cubana.cu | www.cubajet.com (Aerocaribbean)*

ELECTRICITY

More recent hotels have European 220-volt power points, others American 110-volt electric sockets. Bring an adapter!

EMERGENCY

The police emergency number in all of Cuba is 116; in Havana also 106.

HEALTH

No vaccinations are required, unless you enter Cuba from a country where cholera or yellow fever is prevalent. Be careful with water, to avoid stomach or gastric disturbances. Recommended vaccinations include diphtheria, hepatitis A and tetanus. You should have all the medication you need with you in sufficient quantity.

The major tourist hotels have first-aid stations, usually staffed by a doctor, in the tourist areas also international clinics (*www.servimedcuba.com* or contact your embassy). If you need medical attention, pay in cash in CUC. Since 2010, it has been obligatory to have proof of an existing travel health insurance to enter Cuba!

INFORMATION

CUBAN TOURISM AUTHORITY
154 Shaftesbury Avenue | London WC 2H8JT | United Kingdom | tel. 0-207-240 66 55 | tourism@travel2cuba.co.uk | www.autenticacuba.com

1200 Bay St., Suite 305 | Toronto Ontario M5R 2A5 | Canada | tel. 1-416-362-0700 | info@gocuba.ca | www.autenticacuba. com and www.gocuba.ca

INTERNET

There are a few internet cafés and PC terminals in the Etecsa offices and in the post offices, but increasingly guests of the larger hotels are also entitled to free Wi-Fi in the lobbies. Etecsa sells internet cards from 6 CUC with an access code for its usually pretty slow computers.

USEFUL WEBSITES
Official tourism pages:
www.auténticacuba.com

Havana dates:
www.havana-cultura.com

Cuba TV online:
www.cubavision.cubaweb.cu

Cuba radio:
www.radiocubana.cu

Cuba portals (Spanish):
www.cubaweb.cu
www.cuba.cu

MONEY & CURRENCY

Cuba's economy works with two currencies: the Cuban peso (CUP or MN) and the peso convertible (CUC), the Cuban exchange currency, which is worthless abroad. Up to 2004 the US dollar was in circulation as a foreign currency. Now you may exchange US dollars in bureaux de change or banks into CUC, though

you'll pay a ten per cent fee! If you use credit cards, whether in a shop or with your passport at a bank or at ATMs (only with European Visa credit cards and PIN), you will be penalised with a 'credit card fee' and 'dollar exchange' of 11.1124 per cent. The best thing to do is to travel with cash or travellers cheques, as so far cashing them is only subject to a fee of 3 per cent. Careful: if you lose your MasterCard no replacement can be sent to Cuba. Debit cards (EC/Maestro) are not accepted anywhere in Cuba!

In January 2012 1 peso convertible (CUC) bought 22 Cuban pesos (CUP). The national currency can be used by tourists to shop on the farmers markets or at snack stalls.

PERSONAL SAFETY

Sadly, Cuba is no longer the safest Latin American country to travel in. While there are draconian punishments for thieving, assault and bodily harm, they no longer have such an deterrent effect, since corruption is rife. Be careful in lonely areas and with touts who might recommend private accommodation.

PHONE & MOBILE PHONE

The state-run telecommunications company Etecsa runs offices *(daily 8.30am–7.30pm)* and public card phones which you can use to phone abroad. A telephone card *(tarjeta telefónica prepagada)* costs 5, 10 or 20 CUC. For domestic calls, use the local dialling code (with zero), for calls abroad the dialling code 119, then the country code (UK 44, Ireland 353, USA 01), then the local dialling call without the zero. Dialling code for Cuba: 0053.

European mobile/cell phones with a contract will automatically switch to the roaming partner Cubacel. Calls to Europe costs about 5.40 CUC/min. It is possible to hire mobiles/cell phones on Cuba. *www.cubacel.cu*

POST

Stamps can usually be bought together with postcards in the shops, at post offices and in some Etecsa (telephone) offices. An airmail postcard to international destinations costs 0.50 CUC. Mail to the US still travels via Canada or Mexico.

CURRENCY CONVERTER

£	CUC	CUC	£
1	1.60	1	0.62
2	3.20	2	1.23
3	4.85	3	1.85
4	6.50	4	2.50
5	8	5	3.10
7	11.30	6	3.70
8	13	7	4.30
9	14.55	8	5
10	16	9	5.55

$	CUC	CUC	$
1	1	1	1
2	2	2	2
3	3	3	3
4	4	4	4
5	5	5	5
7	7	6	6
8	8	7	7
9	9	8	8
10	10	9	9

For current exchange rates see www.xe.com

PRIVATE ACCOMMODATION

Casas particulares (private houses) are a good-value alternative to the state-run hotels and allow contact with the locals. Addresses and information: *www.cuba-casas.net, www.casaparticularcuba.org.* You'll recognise *casas particulares* by a white sign with a dark-blue icon in the shape of a vertical anchor, usually stuck to the door entrance.

TAXI

The trip from Havana airport into the city costs approx. 25 CUC. The vintage taxis have no taximeter and the fare has to be negotiated. While all other taxis are legally obliged to use the taximeter, many drivers like to switch it off.

TIME

To align with Cuban time, turn the clock back 5 hours compared to Britain.

TIPPING

Instead of making the meagre Cuban salaries (1 CUC = nearly two days' earnings) the yardstick for your tipping policy, it's better to use international standards: so for room service 5 CUC per week, for carrying luggage 2 CUC.

WEATHER IN HAVANA

	Jan	Feb	March	April	May	June	July	Aug	Sept	Oct	Nov	Dec
Daytime temperatures in °C/°F												
	26/79	27/81	28/82	29/84	30/86	31/88	31/88	32/90	31/88	29/84	27/81	26/79
Nighttime temperatures in °C/°F												
	18/64	18/64	19/66	21/70	22/72	23/73	24/75	24/75	24/75	23/73	21/70	19/66
Sunshine hours/day												
	6	6	7	7	8	6	6	6	5	5	5	5
Precipitation days/month												
	6	4	4	4	7	10	9	10	11	11	7	6
Water temperature in °C/°F												
	25/77	24/75	24/75	26/79	27/81	27/81	28/82	28/82	28/82	28/82	27/81	27/81

TRAFFIC

Traffic rules follow more or less western European standards. Cuba drives on the right. Drivers frequently hog the overtaking lane to avoid the many horse-drawn carriages, bikes and pedestrians on the right-hand side of the rural roads. With the exception of a few routes off the beaten track, the roads are overall pretty good. On country roads maximum 90 km/h is allowed, on the motorway (if not otherwise signalled) 100 km/h. *Punto de Control* means checkpoint; make sure you go down to the prescribed 40 km/h! When parking always look for secured spaces *(parqueos)* or look for somebody to guard the car (and pay him), otherwise you might find the radio missing later, a damage that no Cuban insurance will cover.

If involved in an accident where a person is harmed, a tourist has to stay in the country until the recuperation of the injured party is foreseeable or their medical or hospital bills have been paid. This can take up to nine months; you'll have to spend this time in the country at your own cost. Independently of the issue of who was to blame, in cases of accidents where someone was heavily injured or killed, Cuban courts have handed down prison sentences of between 1 and 4 years to foreign drivers.

With accidents (or theft), everything has to be noted and logged by the police for the insurance to pay out. Ask for a copy of the log and make a note of the name of the police officer. Night drives carry a major risk of accidents, as people, cyclists, carriages, cows, mopeds and cars may be travelling on the roads with no lights. Speeding may entail a penalty *(multa)*. However, the police may not take money off drivers; they have to log the fine in the rental car agreement.

The modern 'Servi' stations are open day and night. In 2012 a litre of *especial* (super unleaded) cost 1.30 CUC. You practically always have to pay in cash, even if the petrol station is covered in credit card stickers claiming they are accepted there. The reason given is usually that the credit-card machine is broken or there is no connection.

TRAINS

From the main railway station in Havana, trains depart for the entire country, amongst them three daily night trains from Havana to Santiago de Cuba. Journey time is approx. 12 hrs, *regular* 30 CUC, with air-conditioning from 50 CUC. Tickets are a rare commodity, so it's best to book two weeks ahead; tourist tickets are available from the yellow train station *La Coubre (between the main railway station and port)*. Information: *Ferro cuba | Arsenal/Egido | tel. 07 8 62 80 21,* or timetable information: *tel. 07 62 19 29 | www.hicuba.com/ferrocarril.htm*

USEFUL PHRASES SPANISH

PRONUNCIATION

c	before 'e' and 'i' like 'th' in 'thin'
ch	as in English
g	before 'e' and 'i' like the 'ch' in Scottish 'loch'
gue, gui	like 'get', 'give'
que, qui	the 'u' is not spoken, i.e. 'ke', 'ki'
j	always like the 'ch' in Scottish 'loch'
ll	like 'lli' in 'million'; some speak it like 'y' in 'yet'
ñ	'nj'
z	like 'th' in 'thin'

IN BRIEF

Yes/No/Maybe	sí/no/quizás
Please/Thank you	por favor/gracias
Hello!/Goodbye!/See you	¡Hola!/¡Adiós!/¡Hasta luego!
Good morning!/afternoon!/evening!/night!	¡Buenos días!/¡Buenos días!/¡Buenas tardes!/¡Buenas noches!
Excuse me, please!	¡Perdona!/¡Perdone!
May I ...?/Pardon?	¿Puedo ...?/¿Cómo dice?
My name is ...	Me llamo ...
What's your name?	¿Cómo se llama usted?/¿Cómo te llamas?
I'm from ...	Soy de ...
I would like to .../Have you got ...?	Querría .../¿Tiene usted ...?
How much is ...?	¿Cuánto cuesta ...?
I (don't) like that	Esto (no) me gusta.
good/bad/broken/doesn't work	bien/mal/roto/no funciona
too much/much/little/all/nothing	demasiado/mucho/poco/todo/nada
Help!/Attention!/Caution!	¡Socorro!/¡Atención!/¡Cuidado!
ambulance/police/fire brigade	ambulancia/policía/bomberos
May I take a photo here	¿Podría fotografiar aquí?

DATE & TIME

Monday/Tuesday/Wednesday	lunes/martes/miércoles
Thursday/Friday/Saturday	jueves/viernes/sábado
Sunday/working day/holiday	domingo/laborable/festivo
today/tomorrow/yesterday	hoy/mañana/ayer

¿Hablas español?

"Do you speak Spanish?" This guide will help you to say the basic words and phrases in Spanish

hour/minute/second/moment	hora/minuto/segundo/momento
day/night/week/month/year	día/noche/semana/mes/año
now/immediately/before/after	ahora/enseguida/antes/después
What time is it?	¿Qué hora es?
It's three o'clock/It's half past three	Son las tres/Son las tres y media
a quarter to four/a quarter past four	cuatro menos cuarto/ cuatro y cuarto

TRAVEL

open/closed/opening times	abierto/cerrado/horario
entrance / exit	entrada/acceso salida
departure/arrival	salida/llegada
toilets/ladies/gentlemen	aseos/señoras/caballeros
free/occupied	libre/ocupado
(not) drinking water	agua (no) potable
Where is ...?/Where are ...?	¿Dónde está ...? /¿Dónde están ...?
left/right	izquierda/derecha
straight ahead/back	recto/atrás
close/far	cerca/lejos
traffic lights/corner/crossing	semáforo/esquina/cruce
bus/tram/U-underground/	autobús/tranvía/metro/
taxi/cab	taxi
bus stop/cab stand	parada/parada de taxis
parking lot/parking garage	parking/garaje
street map/map	plano de la ciudad/mapa
train station/harbour/airport	estación/puerto/aeropuerto
ferry/quay	transbordador/muelle
schedule/ticket/supplement	horario/billete/suplemento
single/return	sencillo/ida y vuelta
train/track/platform	tren/vía/andén
delay/strike	retraso/huelga
I would like to rent ...	Querría ... alquilar
a car/a bicycle/a boat	un coche/una bicicleta/un barco
petrol/gas station	gasolinera
petrol/gas / diesel	gasolina/diesel
breakdown/repair shop	avería/taller

FOOD & DRINK

Could you please book a table for tonight for four?	Resérvenos, por favor, una mesa para cuatro personas para hoy por la noche.
on the terrace/by the window	en la terraza/junto a la ventana

The menu, please/	¡El menú, por favor!
Could I please have ...?	¿Podría traerme ... por favor?
bottle/carafe/glass	botella/jarra/vaso
knife/fork/spoon	cuchillo/tenedor/cuchara
salt/pepper/sugar	sal/pimienta/azúcar
vinegar/oil/milk/cream/lemon	vinagre/aceite/leche/limón
cold/too salty/not cooked	frío/demasiado salado/sin hacer
with/without ice/sparkling	con/sin hielo/gas
vegetarian/allergy	vegetariano/vegetariana/alergía
May I have the bill, please?	Querría pagar, por favor.
bill/receipt/tip	cuenta/recibo/propina

SHOPPING

pharmacy/chemist	farmacia/droguería
baker/market	panadería/mercado
butcher/fishmonger	carnicería/pescadería
shopping centre/department store	centro comercial/grandes almacenes
shop/supermarket/kiosk	tienda/supermercado/quiosco
100 grammes/1 kilo	cien gramos/un kilo
expensive/cheap/price/more/less	caro/barato/precio/más/menos
organically grown	de cultivo ecológico

ACCOMMODATION

I have booked a room	He reservado una habitación.
Do you have any ... left?	¿Tiene todavía ...?
single room/double room	habitación individual/habitación doble
breakfast/half board/	desayuno/media pensión/
full board (American plan)	pensión completa
at the front/seafront/garden view	hacia delante/hacia el mar/hacia el jardín
shower/sit-down bath	ducha/baño
balcony/terrace	balcón/terraza
key/room card	llave/tarjeta
luggage/suitcase/bag	equipaje/maleta/bolso
swimming pool/spa/sauna	piscina/spa/sauna
soap/toilet paper/nappy (diaper)	jabón/papel higiénico/pañal
cot/high chair/nappy changing	cuna/trona/cambiar los pañales
deposit	anticipo/caución

BANKS, MONEY & CREDIT CARDS

bank/ATM/	banco/cajero automático/
pin code	número secreto
cash/credit card	en efectivo/tarjeta de crédito
bill/coin/change	billete/moneda/cambio

HEALTH

doctor/dentist/paediatrician	médico/dentista/pediatra
hospital/emergency clinic	hospital/urgencias
fever/pain/inflamed/injured	fiebre/dolor/inflamado/herido
diarrhoea/nausea/sunburn	diarrea/náusea/quemadura de sol
plaster/bandage/ointment/cream	tirita/vendaje/pomada/crema
pain reliever/tablet/suppository	calmante/comprimido/supositorio

POST, TELECOMMUNICATIONS & MEDIA

stamp/letter/postcard	sello/carta/postal
I need a landline phone card/	Necesito una tarjeta telefónica/
I'm looking for a prepaid card for my mobile	Busco una tarjeta prepago para mi móvil
Where can I find internet access?	¿Dónde encuentro un acceso a internet?
dial/connection/engaged	marcar/conexión/ocupado
socket/adapter/charger	enchufe/adaptador/cargador
computer/battery/	ordenador/batería/
rechargeable battery	batería recargable
e-mail address/at sign (@)	(dirección de) correo electrónico/arroba
internet address (URL)	dirección de internet
internet connection/wifi	conexión a internet/wifi
e-mail/file/print	archivo/imprimir

LEISURE, SPORTS & BEACH

beach/sunshade/lounger	playa/sombrilla/tumbona
low tide/high tide/current	marea baja/marea alta/corriente

NUMBERS

0	cero	14	catorce
1	un, uno, una	15	quince
2	dos	16	dieciséis
3	tres	17	diecisiete
4	cuatro	18	dieciocho
5	cinco	19	diecinueve
6	seis	20	veinte
7	siete	100	cien, ciento
8	ocho	200	doscientos, doscientas
9	nueve	1000	mil
10	diez	2000	dos mil
11	once	10000	diez mil
12	doce	1/2	medio
13	trece	1/4	un cuarto

NOTES

MARCO POLO TRAVEL GUIDES

- PACKED WITH INSIDER TIPS
- BEST WALKS AND TOURS
- FULL-COLOUR PULL-OUT MAP
  AND STREET ATLAS

ROAD ATLAS

The green line ▬▬ indicates the Trips & Tours (p. 88–93)
The blue line ▬▬ indicates The perfect route (p. 30–31)

All tours are also marked on the pull-out map

Photo: Trinidad

SYMBOLS

INSIDER TIP   Insider Tip
★   Highlight
●●●●   Best of ...
�🗻   Scenic view

🖤 Responsible travel: fair
  trade principles and the
  environment respected

(*) Telephone numbers that
  are not toll-free

**PRICE CATEGORIES
HOTELS**

Expensive	over 130 CUC
Moderate	60–130 CUC
Budget	under 60 CUC

The prices are for a double
room without breakfast

**PRICE CATEGORIES
RESTAURANTS**

Expensive	over 25 CUC
Moderate	15–25 CUC
Budget	under 15 CUC

The prices are for a menu
(starter, main course, dessert)
without drinks

On the cover: Trip into the colonial past p. 72 | Endless beaches and blue sea p. 55

MARCO POLO

Travel with
**Insider
Tips**

CUBA

USA

Gulf of
Mexico
Havana

BAHAMAS

*ATLANTIC
OCEAN*

MEXICO

CUBA

DOM.
REPUBLIC

JAMAICA

HAITI

BELIZE

HONDURAS

Caribbean Sea

NICARAGUA

VENEZUELA

COLOMBIA

PANAMA

D0493260

www.marco-polo.com